In *Never Stop Praying*, Leo Gafney has achieved a remarkable work: a versatile, spiritual, and practical guide that will inspire a broad readership, including seminarians in training, priests preparing homilies, theology professors, and particularly mature men and women, married or unmarried who want to find God everywhere—from their daily work to the last years of their lives. In 26 chapters, each providing a topic for a week, he takes a single experience—peace, work, sickness, love, forgiveness, the poor, the Holy Spirit—and analyzes it with a passage of Scripture, mental image, and weekly practice that will turn an idea into a character-forming experience and the reader into a more sensitive and living human being.

RAYMOND A. SCHROTH, SJ, *editor emeritus of* **America** *magazine, author of* **The American Jesuits: A History** *and* **The American Journey of Eric Sevareid**

This book gives many practical ways to integrate faith in our lives on a weekly basis. Overall it reminds me of a favorite verse, "Do not conform to the pattern of this world, but be transformed by the renewing of your minds" (Romans 12:2). This book will help ordinary people begin to change their thinking and become transformed on the journey to become more like Jesus.

DICK KIERNAN, *Director of Come Follow Me, a ministry dedicated to "form leaders to make missionary disciples"*

In the midst of our busy, fragmented lives, it is a challenge for Christians to give the necessary attention to their spiritual growth. In *Never Stop Praying*, Leo Gafney skillfully uses meditations on a single word or phrase as a way to focus our attention on our spiritual and moral lives and to allow the Spirit to transform us. This compendium of meditations was, for me, a useful tool in my ongoing search for relationship with God.

KERRY MCKEON ⋯⋯⋯ *petual Help Parish, Washington, CT*

Leo Gafney invites you to take him at his word; and that word is "accept." Accept not just the thoughts he shares with you in this book, but accept as well his invitation to pray your way—randomly perhaps—toward a deeper acceptance of God's love for you. This is a prayer manual that lifts the soul.

WILLIAM J. BYRON, SJ, *author of* **A Book of Quiet Prayer**

With his new book, *Never Stop Praying*, Leo Gafney has offered another fine addition to the growing Catholic library of resources on prayer and spiritual meditation. A genuine pilgrimage with Christ awaits those so inclined.

DEACON RICHARD MAGENIS, *St. Martin of Tours Parish, Canaan, CT*

The commentaries, interspersed with humor and personal reflection, encouraged me to revisit them midweek for further inspiration and to maintain my focus on the specified word. Having a full week allows time for follow-up on Bible passages or other concepts that were mentioned.

DIANA DRAPER, *St. George Catholic Church, Guilford, CT*

For busy people and pastors looking for a user-friendly book about prayer that they can recommend to their parishioners who want to grow closer to God, Leo Gafney has written a first-rate work. Set in the context of twenty-six weeks, he lays out a prayerful week-by-week journey about communicating with God in a very personal way. With a rich commentary on twenty-six themes he provides Scripture readings and weekly practices about how to live more intimately in God's presence on a daily basis. This book is a treasure.

FR. WILLIAM WATTERS, *pastor emeritus, St. Ignatius Church, Baltimore, MD*

NEVER STOP PRAYING

NEVER STOP
praying

WEEKLY MINI-RETREATS
TO GROW YOUR FAITH
EACH DAY

LEO GAFNEY

NEVER STOP
praying

WEEKLY MINI-RETREATS
TO GROW YOUR FAITH
EACH DAY

LEO GAFNEY

TWENTY-THIRD
PUBLICATIONS
twentythirdpublications.com

TWENTY-THIRD PUBLICATIONS
One Montauk Avenue, Suite 200
New London, CT 06320
(860) 437-3012 or (800) 321-0411
www.twentythirdpublications.com

Cover photo: ©shutterstock.com / A. and I. Kruk

ISBN: 978-1-62785-352-1
Library of Congress Control Number: 2017960971
Printed in the U.S.A.

A division of Bayard, Inc.

CONTENTS

INTRODUCTION

We Christians have been blessed in recent years with new books suggesting topics and methods for meditation. These works generally propose settings from the life of Christ and texts from Scripture with explorations to deepen our engagement with God and strengthen our daily living in Christ. Christians have also adapted practices from the Buddhist tradition emphasizing a quieter, less verbal approach as we encounter the spiritual dimensions of our lives. Many Christians start each day with a reading and reflection. Some meditations are based on a single word or phrase.

This book is consistent with current practices on prayer, but instead of emphasizing fifteen- or thirty-minute readings and meditation, I propose a method for cultivating our spiritual lives throughout the day, particularly in the odd moments between our responsibilities and tasks—perhaps while walking or doing other things that leave the mind and heart somewhat free.

This is not to say that the practice of our faith should be squeezed in between the more pressing duties of life, such as

1

work and care for family. Rather, I offer these reflections and exercises with the thought that our faith and understanding of God's work should permeate every aspect of life. It should be like the air we breathe—always there, giving strength to everything we do or encounter—or like the mortar holding together the bricks of a building.

We can quietly control our stray thoughts and feelings, organize them, and use them to grow spiritually. This practice holds an additional advantage in helping us avoid the alternatives—simply letting our minds and hearts wander or, what is worse, drifting into negative thoughts that may promote greed, selfishness, anger, and the many distractions that inhibit spiritual growth. In our wandering minds we are often led to think about things we want or injuries we imagine or ways in which we might get even. And so, controlling and directing our thoughts and images and emotions, we can both avoid evil and seek what is good.

A week seems more suitable to this practice than a day, for several reasons. Days occur naturally with the rising and setting of the sun, while a week is a human invention; still, weeks have a more predictable rhythm. For most of us, weekends are days of relaxation. Sunday for many is still a day for church. Monday to Friday have certain characteristics related to family, work, school, and perhaps volunteer activities. So a week marks out a well-defined unit of time. In addition, a week gives us more time to reflect on the meaning and impact of a word or theme; a day is too short. Finally, some very conscientious Christians who practice daily meditation and frequent prayer have told me that they become anxious and feel guilty if they do not take time for prayer and reflection as often as they believe they should. But living the Christian life should be a source of joy, not guilt. The week may provide a somewhat more leisurely pace to your prayer and reflections, while still maintaining a sense of order.

I will suggest a word or short phrase with ideas about how you might cultivate this for the period of a week. Each meditation concludes with a mental image to which you can quietly return during the day, and also a verse from Scripture to anchor the theme. You might wish to reread the section every morning or several times during the week, thinking about what aspect of it appeals to you or how the word or phrase responds to your needs for the day.

Many people have become serious about their personal development—with exercise, diet, meditation, yoga, and other practices. Again, what is presented here—although we do not prescribe definite times or places—is meant to be taken seriously, and you may want to set aside times and places that are suitable to make your reflections more systematic. But in the spirit of the gospels we leave the practice of faith to the Spirit working within each person.

Each reading also contains a passage from Scripture. There is a depth and warmth in Scripture that reaches the minds and touches the hearts of believers. We are nourished and strengthened in ways that we cannot measure. Just as food and exercise provide the body with strength that will be needed later, so our spiritual strengthening will be needed. In the readings themselves, it might be helpful to proceed slowly, stopping at a word, phrase, or image that seems particularly important to your life and thinking. Allow the love of God to grow quietly in your mind and heart. Some of the Scripture readings are short; I encourage you to go to the chapters listed and read more.

The reflections contained here are only a starting point and will probably be read in the morning or evening. The reading is meant to be a springboard for further thinking and, more importantly, resting your mind, heart, and spirit in God, as guided by the Holy Spirit.

You might of course ask who I am to offer suggestions about spiritual growth. I am a sinner like you, struggling to let God in Christ enter more fully into my life. I have taken only a few steps in this direction; and yet my imperfections, though many, should not prevent me from offering a few insights that may be helpful to others.

Accept

The saints and mystics who have invested years in nourishing their spiritual lives and strengthening their union with God seem always to end by saying that acceptance and surrender are at the core of their being. We can try to do the same.

But it may not be easy. We live in a culture in which "acceptance" is not always welcomed or viewed positively. We are urged to see ourselves in competition with others—in what we do, in how much we earn, in the clothes we wear, even in the accomplishments of our children. Progress and personal growth have become the maxims of our time. Acceptance can be seen as a sign of weakness, dependence, and submission. We may not want to accept compromise, failure, weakness, or even our position in life. We are told we should become something more.

When contemplating the word "accept" as followers of Christ, we find a world very different from the one that surrounds us.

We must begin by accepting ourselves. Christ Our Lord told his followers, and us, to behold the lilies of the field. They neither sow nor reap nor gather into barns, but they are beautiful. God cares for them. Jesus tells us to be like them, to accept God into our lives, and to accept ourselves. You will see flowers, trees, or other growing things many times today. Think of how God cares for them—and how God cares for you.

We are weak; we sin; we are mean to those we love; we fail often; we do not measure up to our own hopes and expectations. Yes, that is who I am and who you are. But God loves us as we are—not as we will be when we have more money, or when our bodies are more attractive, or when we accomplish something wonderful, or even when we are less sinful. When Jesus became human, he took on the weaknesses and limitations of our nature and our world. He accepted who he was with all the disappointments that came with it. In his own town he could not heal because of the people's lack of faith. His closest followers continually misunderstood his message—hoping for an earthly kingdom with worldly power. Christ accepted himself and his world.

In odd moments today and during this week, consider yourself—your body, your mind, your abilities, and your faults—all of you. Accept yourself; God accepts you.

And then as you think of the word "accept," consider those in your life and accept them. Your parents are not perfect; your children are not perfect. Don't worry about changing them. Relax and accept them. They live under the same challenging circumstances and the same kinds of cultural pressures and confusion that you do. Accept them and the others in your life, as they are. They love you and care for you, even more than you know.

There are certainly things that are difficult to accept—losing a job, serious illness, the death of one we love. And yet many of us have experienced God's love and come to a deeper understanding of who we are in these most difficult moments. It is not easy to accept cancer or other life-threatening illnesses. But in dark moments we can come closest to what is at the core of our being, closest to Jesus Christ, who after praying that he might not be asked to face terrible suffering and death, repeated three times to God, "Not my will but yours be done."

We are promised that the Christian life ends in resurrection, in unity with God. And union with God is the reason for all prayer. So we should accept the wonder of God in our lives, and the wonder of our world, and the goodness of those around us. We are never, even for a day, beyond the help that others can bring. We should not be too proud to accept their help. If young, we should accept the guidance and wisdom of those with greater experience; if in the middle of life, we should accept the sharing, companionship, and good fortune of others; if older we should accept our declining strength and the help we need.

Accepting is not always easy, but with practice it can be rewarding. We do not have to strain so hard to see ourselves making progress or to be seen as rich and accomplished in so many ways. Best of all, accepting who we are, accepting God into our lives, and accepting others with all their goodness and all their faults gives us a new freedom.

Strangely, it is perhaps God's love and acceptance that is most difficult for us to accept. We want to judge ourselves harshly. But that is not God's way.

MENTAL IMAGE

Picture Jesus washing the feet of his disciples. They are shocked. Peter resists. Jesus proceeds quietly, telling them that they will understand.

SCRIPTURE READING

This week's reading is from the Gospel of John, chapter 13. In this chapter, we read what should be the ultimate source of acceptance. Jesus is the way to the Father, and we are connected to Jesus. In many ways, our faith will surprise us, as Jesus surprised his disciples.

> Then he poured water into a basin and began to wash the disciples' feet and to wipe them with the towel that was tied around him. He came to Simon Peter, who said to him, "Lord, are you going to wash my feet?" Jesus answered, "You do not know now what I am doing but later you will understand." Peter said to him, "You will never wash my feet." Jesus answered, "Unless I wash you, you have no share with me." Simon Peter said to him, "Lord, not my feet only but also my hands and my head!" Jesus said to him, "One who has bathed does not need to wash, except for the feet, but is entirely clean." JOHN 13:5–10

SCRIPTURE VERSE

"So if I, your Lord and Teacher, have washed your feet, you also ought to wash one another's feet." JOHN 13:14

At the end of these meditations we will offer one or more suggestions to further focus the mind and heart and move to a deeper commitment. If you are so inclined, writing your reflections, commitments, and concerns might be helpful.

WEEKLY PRACTICE

Write down or fix in your mind one thing that you find particularly difficult to accept about yourself. It may be a quick temper, or a lack of sympathy for others, or a bit of stinginess. We are not talking about serious sins but areas of life that we are not quite satisfied with. Don't make any great resolutions to change. Accept yourself. But know yourself.

Toward midweek: Write down several ways in which you feel more free and happy because you have accepted yourself with your faults, as God accepts you.

At the end of the week: Write a very brief prayer asking God to help you accept the work of the Spirit in your life.

WEEK

2

Peace

T he refrain for a hymn we sing in church proclaims, "Let there be peace on earth, and let it begin with me." For some reason—perhaps the words, perhaps the melody—the refrain sounds a bit too precious when sung. But as a basis for reflection from time to time during the week, it can work very well. I am not the center of the universe, and I am very unlikely to achieve something really big. But in small ways you and I can initiate moments of peace—for ourselves and for others—throughout the day. This week, let peace begin with you.

Peace is, in the first instance, a lack or cessation of conflict. Many of the petty arguments that punctuate our days are about something other than what the words are saying. A discussion about politics may start with differences about the role of public agencies and private enterprise, for example, but quickly deteriorate into sarcasm and comments that are made more to dominate and win a point, or even to embarrass, rather than to honestly look for the truth or the best course of action. In the same way, a discussion about which restaurant to visit or which movie to watch can quickly have a subtext about who is in charge, who is making the decisions. But: "Let peace begin with me."

A few days ago, as I drove past a landmark inn in our town, eight or ten people with signs for peace waved to the cars going past. These and others in the towns near us can be seen on weekends in quiet vigil. They remind us of the larger world where weapons are multiplying and killing is the solution to many problems. We live in a democracy, and in some small way each of us can play a role promoting peace beyond ourselves.

After several of his healings, Jesus said, "Your faith has saved you; go in peace" (see, for example, Mark 5:34). It seems not only that the healing ended the person's troubles, but engagement with Jesus brought these people to a new level of rest and quietness of spirit. That engagement is still available. The Spirit of God dwells within us, ready to bring a deeper sense of peace. It doesn't take a great deal of effort. During this week, accept the peace that God brings.

In Luke's gospel, when Jesus, after his resurrection, first appeared to the disciples assembled and confused, he said, "Peace be with you" (Luke 24:36), and then he asked why they were startled and terrified. They were terrified in part because they thought they were in the presence of a ghost. But even for us, contact with God in Christ can be frightening. "Do I really believe? Am I able or willing to commit to the challenges that God asks of me? Do I want to be taken beyond what I can see and hear?" The answer of course is that the peace of Christ and our faith do enable us to live our lives in God.

In his last discourse in John's gospel Jesus says, "Peace I leave with you; My peace I give to you. I do not give to you as the world gives" (John 14:27). In thinking about this promise, we come to understand that the peace given by Jesus is much more than the lack of conflict. The world might give that sort of peace, only to take it away again. The peace of Christ is quietness of soul. We rest in God's love and in the assurance that nothing can separate us from that love.

And so we can paradoxically retain peace in the midst of unavoidable conflict. Problems with money, sickness, and personal relationships can be troubling, but they should not take away the peace that is in our hearts. Divers report that even when there are tumultuous storms at sea, deep down there remains a calm untroubled world. So it should be in our hearts.

Sometimes peace overtakes us unexpectedly. It may begin with a wonderful view of mountains or the sea; it may seem to be the result of a warm and reassuring conversation. But we should rest in that peace. God works through natural things to touch our hearts. And if we return to that peace, asking God's help to retain that view, and in times of disturbance to guide us as we make that dive below the surface, we will be refreshed. We will also be able to help others to find peace. For peace to live in our hearts, it must be shared. Like love, the more we give away, the more we have—so it is with peace.

MENTAL IMAGE

Jesus talks with his disciples at the Last Supper. He expresses great love for them and promises peace.

SCRIPTURE READING

In this reading, Jesus tells his followers that he is leaving, but the Spirit, the Advocate, will be with them, bringing peace. This peace is not the peace that the world gives. In other words, it is not the peace that might come from financial security, good health, or successful children. The peace of Christ goes deeper into our souls, and cannot be taken away.

> "I have said these things to you while I am still with
> you. But the Advocate, the Holy Spirit, whom the
> Father will send in my name, will teach you every-

thing, and remind you of all that I have said to you.
Peace I leave with you; my peace I give to you. I do not
give to you as the world gives. Do not let your hearts
be troubled, and do not let them be afraid. You heard
me say to you, 'I am going away, and I am coming
to you.' If you loved me, you would rejoice that I am
going to the Father, because the Father is greater than
I. And now I have told you this before it occurs, so that
when it does occur, you may believe." JOHN 14:25–29

SCRIPTURE VERSE

"Peace I leave with you; my peace I give to you." JOHN 14:27

WEEKLY PRACTICE

Think of those things that tend to disturb your peace; think
then about how insignificant they are compared with the peace
of Christ that has been granted to you. Write down one or two
of the things that worry you, taking away your peace. Just seeing
them in writing will help you see how small they are compared
with the peace in your soul.

During the week: Look for opportunities to bring a moment of
peace to someone you know or even someone you meet casually.
Pray that God's peace may become more active in your life and
that peace might begin with you.

Sickness

St. Ignatius Loyola wrote that his followers in the Jesuits should, "thank God for sickness seeing it is no less a gift than health." This advice is not easy to take. When sick, we want to be restored to health.

But Ignatius spoke from experience. He was wounded in battle, his leg badly broken by a cannonball. Recovery took the better part of a year, and was interrupted once when he insisted that the leg be re-broken and set again because he did not want to be left with a limp. This happened anyway.

But while recuperating, the only reading materials available to Ignatius were stories from the life of Christ and the lives of saints. He read these repeatedly, and then he analyzed his own reflections. He found that when thinking of returning to the life of a soldier and libertine, he was left feeling dry and unsatisfied. But when he thought about following Jesus more closely, he was left encouraged and at peace.

And so when Ignatius taught his followers to thank God for sickness and physical ill fortune, he undoubtedly had in mind his own prolonged recovery from wounds received in battle and his subsequent conversion and new life, with the founding of the Society of Jesus. This may not have happened if he had not been wounded and forced to suffer during a long recovery.

You and I have heard people talk about how a battle with cancer or a heart attack had been blessings. Why? Because the people afflicted were forced, like Ignatius, to take a break from their day-to-day lives and think about what was more important, to consider their many blessings, to rededicate themselves to their families and perhaps change what was going wrong, and to live more Christian lives. Things, perhaps like money and looking good, that had been important, now seemed trivial. So while we may not be inclined to ask for illness or injury, we might indeed thank God when these come to us and ask that they be the means for us to review and reform our lives.

One of the first things Peter did, after being chosen by Jesus and accepting the invitation to change his life, was to invite Jesus to his home, to meet the family. We don't know whether Peter had children, but he did have a wife and mother-in-law.

> After leaving the synagogue he entered Simon's house:
> Now Simon's mother-in-law was suffering from a
> high fever, and they asked him about her. Then he
> stood over her and rebuked the fever and it left her.
> Immediately she got up and began to serve them.
> LUKE 4:38–39

Up to this point in Luke's gospel, the first disciples had seen Jesus drive out an "unclean demon," rebuking it. In the incident described above, "they asked him about her." This is an interesting phrase. The disciples were getting to know Jesus. We would like to know more. Did they ask whether she would die of the fever? Or whether they should call a doctor? Or whether he could do something about it?

In any case, Jesus immediately healed her, and she got up and headed for the kitchen. Sometimes a sickness can provide a welcome break, particularly as we begin to regain strength from a flu or bad cold. The enforced rest can be helpful, taking us away from our daily routine and responsibilities.

Anthony DeMello reported that he observed many men who, when diagnosed with AIDS, suddenly found deep inner peace. It seems that facing death told them they no longer had to worry about all the anxieties that accompany life. Serious illness in ourselves or in the ones we love does provide a fresh perspective.

There is another dimension to our reflections on sickness—that is of course our response to others who are sick. We can help in the healing process. I have a friend who does not ask what she can do for one who is sick and in need; she simply does it—bringing a meal, stopping for a visit, running an errand, taking care of the children. There are so many things that must be done that we have trouble attending to when we are not well. When sick, we become frail, uncertain, and unsure of everything around us. The warmth and assurance of a friend can be of very great value.

Cardinal Bernardin suggested that we pray regularly and earnestly while we are well, because prayer is difficult when the body is weakened by sickness or in pain. None of us likes to think about being sick. But sickness and weakness will come to us, and we can prepare. We don't know just how we will respond to serious illness. One doctor friend said that when ill we tend to become more of what we are. In other words, those who are impatient or argumentative become more so. Those who are by nature more resigned tend to accept illness. But some people surprise us. Perhaps there is something deep down within us that sickness reaches. And perhaps this is why people can benefit so much from serious illness.

MENTAL IMAGE

Picture yourself sick or otherwise suffering and in need of God's care.

SCRIPTURE READING

Paul relates mystical revelations that transported him beyond this world. He then describes a "thorn," that keeps him humble. We don't know what this refers to. Some have suggested a chronic illness of the eyes. We don't have the extremes in our spiritual lives that Paul describes. But all of us have our own difficulties that seem to get in the way of the lives we want to live. But we should see them as part of the spiritual journey—a sign of God's love and presence that can help keep us focused on our need for God.

> I know a person in Christ who fourteen years ago was caught up to the third heaven—whether in the body or out of the body I do not know; God knows. And I know that such a person—whether in the body or out of the body I do not know; God knows—was caught up into Paradise and heard things that are not to be told, that no mortal is permitted to repeat....Therefore to keep me from being too elated, a thorn was given me in the flesh, a messenger of Satan to torment me, to keep me from being too elated. Three times I appealed to the Lord about this that it would leave me, but he said to me, "My grace is sufficient for you, for power is made perfect in weakness." 2 CORINTHIANS 12:2–4; 7–9

SCRIPTURE VERSE

Three times I appealed to the Lord about this that it would leave me, but he said to me, "My grace is sufficient for you, for power is made perfect in weakness." 2 CORINTHIANS 12:8–9

WEEKLY PRACTICE

Write in your journal about the darkness you sometimes feel when sick or when a friend is sick or has died. Then write about how incomprehensible God is, and about how your life is shaped by things far beyond your understanding.

Faith

Faith, belief, and trust in a God who cares and is approachable, a God who saves through Jesus Christ—this faith is the foundation of the Christian life. Think and pray this week about what it means to have faith.

A woman came close to Jesus as he walked, surrounded by a crowd. She hoped that if she could but touch his cloak she would be cured from a long-standing affliction. It seems she was afraid to present herself, and the gospel says she had already spent all her money seeking cures. She did touch him, and she was cured. Jesus stopped and turned and spoke, "Who touched my clothes?" His disciples asked how he could wonder who touched him. The crowd surrounded him, with people touching him at every step. The woman came forward and fell down in fear. Jesus said, "Daughter, your faith has made you well; go in peace, and be healed of your disease" (Mark 5:34).

Faith, believing, can cure us—not of our diseases, but more importantly of our weakness of spirit, our tendency to look for happiness in the wrong places. The Spirit of God wants to be engaged in your life more fully this week, today in particular.

In the letters of the apostle Paul, it is faith that brings God's saving work in Christ into the lives of believers. Paul insisted that the old law had been fulfilled. We are made right with God now, not through the rules and regulations that the Jews tried to follow, not through circumcision, not by eating or refraining from certain foods, but by believing the teachings, life, death, and resurrection of Jesus Christ.

In the Acts of the Apostles, members of the early church are called simply "believers." Their lives were transformed by faith in Christ. And they lived that faith in community, caring for one another.

Believing does not mean that the commandments are no longer important or that we do not strive to avoid evil. With God's help, in faith, we can maintain our lives in justice and in charity. Since the early church there have been discussions about the role of faith and works in our lives. There is a kind of tension. We truly believe that Christ himself and our faith in him have changed our lives and made us right with God. But we also know that in the great last judgment scene in the Gospel of Matthew (chapter 25), all are judged by what they have done for others in their times of need.

There is no contradiction between faith and good works. As faith becomes a stronger foundation for our lives we will work more generously for others. Jesus said that faith even the size of a tiny seed could move mountains. This is because faith connects us to God. But nurturing even a little faith is not easy. A man in need, perhaps in tears, seeking help for his son, said to Jesus, "I believe; help my unbelief" (Mark 9:24). We should say the same, frequently, this week.

Think and pray this week about how your faith can better show itself. Living your faith will also strengthen it.

But faith is always mixed with doubt. We live in a world that celebrates the success of science. We do not need God to explain the weather or diseases or wars. Many people ridicule faith and belief in God: all the more reason for our faith. Faith is not a matter of believing that there is a God. For us, this is a given. Nor does faith mean simply accepting a list of dogmas. No, faith is deeply personal and, at the same time, deeply communal.

Our faith can be tested. Disease may strike us or those we love. We are disappointed by betrayals; we see children dying in seemingly needless ways. These have always been part of life. But pain and death and disappointment do not separate us from the God within and beyond us. They can bring us closer to God in faith, because they help put us in contact with a world beyond space and time.

Still, we are surrounded by a secular world in which many say very plainly that they do not want faith; they want to use human reasoning to understand and deal with the world. The only problem with this is that reason and science cannot explain what is most important. Some of those who live without faith find that their lives are meaningless. We all yearn for something beyond us. We are destined for life with and in God, here and now and in the future. Faith gives us the strength and clarity to live in love and in peace—with Christ, in God, and with the help of the Spirit.

Faith must grow in our lives or it will decay. Prayer, Scripture, concern for others, working to build the community—these will strengthen and build faith in us as individuals and as community.

During the day, consider how lucky we are to have the great works of Jesus in our lives. Your faith will be tested, perhaps even ridiculed. But as we nurture the great gift of faith, our lives become richer, simpler. God Our Father, though distant, is near.

MENTAL IMAGE

Picture the crowds around Jesus and the woman timidly pushing through just to touch his cloak.

SCRIPTURE READING

This passage from the Letter to the Hebrews contains what has often been cited as the biblical definition of faith. After this general statement, the author describes the faith of those in the Old Testament and finally comes to Jesus. Did Jesus need faith? He was fully human and so I think we can say that like us he needed faith to grow in his life with God.

> Now faith is the assurance of things hoped for, the conviction of things not seen. Indeed, by faith our ancestors received approval. By faith we understand that the worlds were prepared by the word of God, so that what is seen was made from things that are not visible....
>
> Therefore, since we are surrounded by so great a cloud of witnesses, let us also lay aside every weight and the sin that clings so closely, and let us run with perseverance the race that is set before us, looking to Jesus the pioneer and perfecter of our faith, who for the sake of the joy that was set before him endured the cross, disregarding its shame, and has taken his seat at the right hand of the throne of God.
>
> HEBREWS 11:1–3; 12:1–2

SCRIPTURE VERSE

Now faith is the assurance of things hoped for. HEBREWS 11:1

WEEKLY PRACTICE

Think of a recent time in your life when you really needed faith, and it was there—because faith is a gift from God.

During the week: Consider some of the doubts that surround your faith. These doubts are not bad; they come with faith. Say the prayer, "I do believe; Lord, help my unbelief."

Toward the end of the week: Write a message to God giving thanks for some special reason you have to be grateful for the gift of faith.

Prayer

Prayer, more than anything else, separates the one who believes in God from the one who does not. We who believe find that prayer engages us with that mystery deep within us and infinitely beyond us. In prayer we surrender ourselves to the Love that holds together all of reality. It is through prayer that we find meaning and direction in our lives, and in one another. The purpose of all prayer is union with God—to strengthen our union with God.

For the nonbeliever, prayer often looks like an exercise in which we talk to ourselves or pretend to be in touch with some super-powerful being who is in fact not there. Yes, many atheists and agnostics admit that there are mysteries, even that there is a deep-down reality that holds things together. But to imagine that we can communicate with this mystery makes no sense to them.

And yet it is probably also true that many believers pray mindlessly offering words without soul, and that many non-believers do in fact engage with that deeper reality to which we all belong. So it may not be as easy as we at first think to say who and who is not a person of prayer. And in any case, it is surely not for me or you to judge the prayer life of others. Let us rather consider the different kinds of prayer in our own lives.

Adoration and Awe

In the first verses of Psalms 104 and 105 we are caught up in the psalmist's sense of wonder and awe at the natural world. Further on, Psalm 104 praises God for the things that are around us and that are part of our lives.

> You cause the grass to grow for the cattle,
>   and plants for people to use,
> to bring forth food from the earth,
>   and wine to gladden the human heart,
> oil to make the face shine,
>   and bread to strengthen the human heart.
>
> PSALM 104:14–15

To the beauty of the natural world we can add the sense of wonder we feel when experiencing works of art and music. In a sunset or mountain vista or Mozart symphony we are caught up in something beyond us. In our hearts we say, "how great thou art." Or perhaps even without words we experience that there is more than this material world, this day-to-day life, and we praise God.

Asking for Help

Prayer of petition is problematic, primarily because so many prayers seem to go unanswered. We ask for God's healing presence in time of sickness, for ourselves or for others—and nothing seems to happen. We pray that our children will be safe and yet some die young and others are mistreated. More broadly, when we look at the newspaper or television news it seems that disaster follows disaster with little reason. The starvation and misery in some parts of the world are more than we want to look at or consider. What kind of world is this? Is this the best that God can do?

As is always the case, we have to look to Jesus and others whose lives were totally given to God to gain a deeper understanding of prayers of petition, asking God for—for what? Jesus told Peter that he prayed that his faith might be strengthened. Paul echoes this prayer many times in his letters. Many times in the New Testament we are told to pray that we may not fail in times of temptation. Jesus told us to ask God for bread each day. He himself prayed that he not have to suffer as the end was coming, but immediately turned the situation over to his Father.

What can we learn? First, our lives must be rooted in the unshakable conviction that we are connected to God and engaged in an eternal enterprise that is building the kingdom of God. Sickness, pain, suffering, and death are among the building blocks of this kingdom. Everything in our tradition, from Jesus and Paul to the countless martyrs, and on to Pope Francis, teach us to trust in the love and providence of God— while working with all of our strength and commitment to build the kingdom of God.

We are part of a community—a community of faith and a world of people committed to what is best within each of us. When children are starving in Africa or mistreated in our midst, we should be concerned. We should try in whatever way we can to ease suffering, to bring health, and to commit ourselves to building a world in which justice and peace thrive. God is within us; as individuals and as community, God works with us.

Repentance

We are saved by the work of Christ. We have become new creatures, accepted with all our faults by God, and so we should be happy, experiencing the freedom of the children of God. And yet, as Dietrich Bonhoeffer points out, it seems that in many ways we still live in the Old Testament. We witness unspeakable evil—on both a small and large scale. We find evil within us. All through the Scriptures—old and new—we are told to repent, to turn away from sin and toward God.

Many Christians over the centuries have found solace in one of the most ancient of prayers, the Jesus prayer: "Lord Jesus Christ, Son of God, have mercy on me a sinner." Many have found a unique power and comfort in this prayer—in repeating it over and over. We are saved, but we are sinful. God loves us, but we repent our waywardness. Life is full of paradoxes.

Prayers of Thanks

It is the sense of gratitude that often melts the hurt, troubled, or hardened heart. When illness or financial misfortune strikes, the Spirit of God within us often prompts a prayer out of our own depths, telling us, "You have much to be thankful for." At these times we often think of our generally good health or our generally kind and loving friends, or the good things around us. But we should go deeper. It is our connection to God and to all of creation, to the mysterious love that connects us—for these things we should give thanks. It is most of all our life in Christ for which we should give thanks, remembering his prayer.

> At that same hour, Jesus rejoiced in the Holy Spirit and said, "I thank you, Father, Lord of heaven and earth, because you have hidden these things from the wise and intelligent, and have revealed them to infants; yes, Father, for such was your gracious will."
> LUKE 10:21

MENTAL IMAGE

Jesus at prayer.

SCRIPTURE READING

Psalm 8 is a quiet but powerful message of wonder. We humans are seen in one verse as insignificant and in the next as very close to God.

> What are human beings that you are mindful of them,
>> mortals that you care for them?
> Yet you have made them a little lower than God,
>> and crowned them with glory and honor.
> You have given them dominion over the works
>>> of your hands;
>> you have put all things under their feet,
> all sheep and oxen,
>> and also the beasts of the field,
> the birds of the air, and the fish of the sea,
>> whatever passes along the paths of the seas.
> O Lord, our Sovereign,
>> how majestic is your name in all the earth!
>
> PSALM 8:4–9

SCRIPTURE VERSE

I will give thanks to the Lord with my whole heart. PSALM 111:1

WEEKLY PRACTICE

Read and contemplate Psalm 8 each morning.

Words

We are accustomed to believe that actions speak louder than words. And while this is often true, particularly when promises are kept with actions, we should not underrate the importance of words. Poetry can lift our minds and hearts so that we see and feel the world around us in a new way. A sincere compliment can provide us with strength and sense of purpose when needed. A carefully reasoned discussion can deepen our understanding— of human behavior, the natural world, and of life itself.

In the first verses of the Book of Genesis we read, "God said, 'Let there be light.'" And in the rest of the chapter, God creates with words alone. In the first verse of the Gospel of John, we read, "In the beginning was the Word." Jesus is described as the Word of God. He is the perfect word—a message and more than a message. A word represents a thing. If I say "tree" or "ship" you picture in your mind a tree or a ship. Jesus Christ gives us the image of God—in his teachings, his actions, his compassion, his suffering, and his resurrection. He shows us what God must be like. And so, it is not surprising that Jesus Christ himself is the Word, the representation of God for us.

The understanding of God that we gain from Jesus, the Word, is not what most religions and peoples have found in their ideas of God. Jesus, the Word of God, did not come into the world and does not come into our hearts with power and force. Rather, he comes as gently as a ray of morning sun, or the dew on the grass. He comes to us willingly—that is, he wills it, and he depends on our willingness.

The mystic Meister Eckhart tells us that we also were there when God first conceived the Word. We were and are in the mind and heart of God. We reflect the goodness and compassion of God. This is powerful matter for reflection. How can we more fully and more energetically bring the love and compassion that is within us to those we meet today?

Lawyers and judges take words very seriously. The meanings of words and phrases in our constitution have been debated, and courts' decisions often have a profound impact on people's lives. Contracts, patents, and copyright agreements control the flow of millions of dollars. And in our private lives, the words of marriage contracts and even everyday promises are of great value.

Promises are important. Children take them seriously: Do you promise—to take me to the beach, to buy me the toy or game that I want? Perhaps we should make more promises, even to ourselves in the quiet of our hearts. This week, let us consider the importance of words—as we speak and as we listen, and as we reflect on the words of Scripture.

This week, today, consider your words. Plan to say something that will help heal or encourage someone who needs help. Think about your words after you speak. Notice if your words are helping to bond you more closely to those you love.

MENTAL IMAGE

Jesus as a little child learning to speak from his mother, listening to her, and repeating the word.

SCRIPTURE READING

James in this letter describes the power of words, comparing them to other small things that have great effect.

> Not many of you should become teachers, my brothers and sisters, for you know that we who teach will be judged with greater strictness. For all of us make many mistakes. Anyone who makes no mistakes in speaking is perfect, able to keep the whole body in check with a bridle. If we put bits into the mouths of horses to make them obey us, we guide their whole bodies. Or look at ships: though they are so large that it takes strong winds to drive them, yet they are guided by a very small rudder wherever the will of the pilot directs. So also the tongue is a small member, yet it boasts of great exploits. JAMES 3:1–5

SCRIPTURE VERSE

In the beginning was the Word and the Word was with God and the Word was God. JOHN 1:1

WEEKLY PRACTICE

We often say things that we have heard in order to appear knowledgeable or insightful. This week, listen closely to what you are saying. Ask yourself why you are saying what you say. Try from time to time during the week to think about what you will say to help someone, to comfort and support them.

Write in your journal some words from Scripture that have been helpful to you this week.

Patience

God demonstrated extraordinary patience in creating and nurturing the universe. I say that because creation is best considered as a work-in-progress. Since the Big Bang and its colossal release of energy the universe has been taking shape for more than thirteen billion years. During that time, according to the best estimates now available, at least one hundred to two hundred billion galaxies have taken shape. And each galaxy contains hundreds of billions of stars. Our solar system and our Earth are more than four billion years old.

Does this mean anything to us as Christians? Non-believers sometimes offer these facts and figures as evidence that there is no God, or if there is some Mystery behind the universe, it surely cannot involve us in any personal way. Some believers seem to use similar reasoning to deny the age of the universe, or to deny an evolution that does not work as they think it should. They find it difficult to accept a universe of the size and age that science has found and that contradicts a literal reading of the Bible. But who are we to pass judgment on the creator? God took a long time and let the universe unfold in its own way. These facts should not embarrass or confuse us. The world of the Spirit is not dwarfed by space and time.

Disputes also arise in discussions of evolution. The fact is that by the best available scientific thinking, mutations take place in a random way. Then those mutations that create beneficial changes tend to survive. And, of course, some mutations create deficiencies, disease, and even death. Why should this be scandalous? The process of random mutations is a plan that has worked. Is the universe less beautiful or wonderful because it has developed in this painstaking way? Or is it all the more wonderful? Some people cannot accept a God whose work proceeds through trial and error. Why not?

As you observe nature today or think about the evolution of the universe and of human life, think also about the wonder that is the human mind. But this same mind should not stand in judgment of God simply because God is beyond our understanding.

God has also shown extraordinary patience in working with humankind. God knew and knows that we as individuals and as a human race must proceed slowly, again by trial and error. We learn a little, we pass it on to others; we forget; we make mistakes. That is the way our lives and our learning proceed. And such is the way God reveals the divine plan to us, the way we should come to God.

There are many stories in Scripture about how God works slowly, waiting, helping people understand and gradually to accept God's way of thinking. God made promises to Abraham that in a way stand for what most people want—to be part of something more than themselves, to be part of a family, a people, and to have roots in the land. But it took a very long time for Abraham to achieve what God had promised.

God also showed considerable patience with the people of Israel as they followed but also strayed from the path set for them. They were often obstinate in their pilgrimage toward understanding and following the way of the Lord. But they also produced wonderful prayers, the Psalms, and offered inspiration in the words of prophets.

Jesus also exhibited tireless patience in his encounters with people, particularly those he selected to follow him most closely. Jesus' teachings were about a God whose love is…patient. God waits for us; God wants our love and devotion, but God does not force things. We as a people have continually misunderstood. But God rarely showed anger. God knew that deeper understanding would take time.

This week, as you contemplate the patience of God and the patience that Jesus demonstrated, think about what it means to you. God is waiting each day for you to give yourself more fully. God is patient.

And can we imitate the patience of Christ, our Lord? If you have children or work with children, they will try your patience, but only because they are learning. And like the evolution of the universe, and of life on earth, it all proceeds by trial and error, and trying again. When children are learning to walk and talk, it is usually not difficult to be patient; we see that they are trying and succeeding. Something similar is happening when they are older and perhaps making other kinds of mistakes. They need guidance but also patience.

We should be patient with our spouses, friends, and coworkers. We should treat others as we would like to be treated. And we should be patient with ourselves. The universe was not formed in a day. If you are trying to acquire a new skill or to learn something about your job, or—whatever it might be—be patient with yourself. God is near and God is patient.

MENTAL IMAGE

Imagine a seed in the ground, nurtured by the soil around it and by the water that seeps down to it; very slowly the seed begins to sprout and the sprout begins to grow—to become a flower or vegetable or great tree. Nature works patiently.

SCRIPTURE READING

Psalm 136 reminds us of God's patience and steadfast love in the world, in our lives, and in history.

> O give thanks to the Lord, for he is good,
>> for his steadfast love endures forever.
> O give thanks to the God of gods,
>> for his steadfast love endures forever.
> O give thanks to the Lord of lords,
>> for his steadfast love endures forever;
> who alone does great wonders,
>> for his steadfast love endures forever;
> who by understanding made the heavens,
>> for his steadfast love endures forever;
> who spread out the earth on the waters,
>> for his steadfast love endures forever;
> who made the great lights,
>> for his steadfast love endures forever;
> the sun to rule over the day,
>> for his steadfast love endures forever;
> the moon and stars to rule over the night,
>> for his steadfast love endures forever.

PSALM 136:1–9

SCRIPTURE VERSE

*O give thanks to the Lord, for he is good,
    for his steadfast love endures forever.* PSALM 136:1

WEEKLY PRACTICE

Think about times when you needed someone to be patient toward you and they were patient.

Be patient with someone who "tries your patience."

8

Symbols and Rituals

ecause we are human, body and spirit intertwined, we are compelled to go beyond ourselves—to seek and find hidden worlds and meanings that we feel deeply but only dimly recognize and barely understand. So we use signs that point to truths that are buried within our hearts and also take us beyond our imaginings.

My wife loves to receive flowers. They bring beauty to the house but also symbolize love renewed, promises made and kept, and mutual concern. Like many men I joke that flowers don't last. A joke, and yet perhaps there is a hidden truth in this as well.

In a very beautiful poem, Edmund Waller compares his love to a rose. He bids the rose go to his beloved and tell her that if it had sprung up in the desert, its beauty would have gone unnoticed. He tells the rose to bid her come forth, "suffer herself to be desired." The poem concludes with a reminder of mortality.

37

Then die, that she
The common fate of all things rare
Might see in thee:
How small a part of time they share
That are so wondrous, sweet, and fair!

Life is sweet and fair, and yet we must die. The poetry above might be said to be marks on paper. But we are human and therefore able to invest meaning and energy, perhaps even tears, into the poem.

Words are extraordinarily powerful symbols. Based on words, people dedicate their lives to one another or to God, fortunes change hands, wars break out, and peace may be achieved. It is a big mistake to take words lightly.

Beyond things and words we use actions as signs. Daily, we extend a kiss or handshake or wave to friends and acquaintances. The handshake, once a brief check to ascertain that neither party was armed, is now a sign of respect and good will—often an indication of willingness to work together or to close a deal. Think this week about the importance of signs, symbols, and rituals in your life.

Another brief ritual is the toast, usually with wine. Many people never take a drink without at least a very brief, "Cheers," or "To your health," or to some special event. We might feel a bit uneasy when people begin to drink their wine without this mutual recognition of a common bond, some effort to acknowledge that we are doing more than just eating and drinking. We are together as people with a destiny beyond taking care of our bodies.

Societies living closer to nature often have elaborate rituals in which they link the mundane with the spiritual. You have no doubt read about Native Americans dancing in preparation for the hunt. The dancers act out the hunt, displaying the search for the bison, the fear and respect in the encounter, and finally the conquest. The dance, music, and song prepare the hunters and the people generally for the action, providing them with courage, skill, and excitement, and linking them with ages past. In a way that cannot be explained, the ritual also connects them with the unseen power that unites the hunter and the hunted.

The natural impulse to use signs and symbols became a most important element in the religious expression of the people of Israel. As a nation, as families, and as individuals, they wanted to show their total commitment as a covenant people. This began with the circumcision of males, which is a ritual and a clear physical reminder of the commitment.

The offering of sacrifice is another recurring religious ritual. The animals offered in thanksgiving and in expiation for sin were burned with the conviction that the smell of the burnt offering would be pleasing to God, and that the people might be accepted, that their union with God would be strengthened.

The Seder reenacts the meal before the flight from slavery in Egypt. It reminds families, with carefully prescribed prayers, readings, and foods, that they have been saved by the Lord and must continue to live according to the promises and commandments of the Lord.

There were also ritual washings, such as the baptism of John, in which God was called on to cleanse and refresh those who came forward, acknowledging their sinfulness and calling for help. Think this week about the rituals in your life and how you might introduce additional small reminders of your spiritual journey. Children can learn from and take comfort in small family rituals—a phrase used in saying good night, or prayers before dinner. Coworkers and friends can seal relationships with small, unexpected gifts.

The prophets of Israel spoke often and eloquently about the importance of internal commitment of mind and heart. This, they proclaimed, is what is truly pleasing to God, more than the burnt offerings of animals or grain. It is this spirit of total commitment, totally lived, that infused Jesus, the Lord.

As the perfect one of God, Jesus summarized in himself all of the dedication of his people. His life, his teaching, his miracles, and finally his death and resurrection were pleasing to God, and so his life is the sign and the sacrament for a new people.

This sacrament, which is Christ, points in two directions. Christ, coming from the Father, shows us that God himself is able to love in a way that includes suffering and sacrifice. In fact, it is this love that is at the center of all that is good. Then, Christ turns and, as one of us, shows the Father that he has claimed us, that in spite of all our sinfulness and selfishness he cares for us and has even sent the Spirit of love to be with us, guiding and inspiring our lives.

We do not find God directly, although we must pray and accept the inner guidance that he gives. We do not meet Christ directly, although we must embrace his message and strive with the help of the Spirit to live in his image. But we find out what it means to be Christians through the very humbling experience of living in the church, among the holy and sinful people called together by Christ, and who continue to live as his body.

The church, then, has been called a sacrament because she is meant, like Christ, to be a sign and instrument of communion with God and of unity among people. She speaks to her people and beyond about the amazing self-giving of God, of how God creates, forgives, brings new life, and showers never ending love on creatures. The church then turns and, with the unceasing prayers of the body of Christ, tells the Father that we are trying, we are sorry, we do believe.

MENTAL IMAGE

Jesus talking with his first disciples.

SCRIPTURE READING

In this week's reading from the Gospel of John, several important signs and symbols are used to describe moments in the early ministry of Jesus: Jesus is called the "Lamb of God." He changes Simon's name. These incidents are recalled with loving memory. The evangelist looks back on those first very important times.

> The next day John again was standing with two of
> his disciples, and as he watched Jesus walk by, he
> exclaimed, "Look, here is the Lamb of God!" The two
> disciples heard him say this, and they followed Jesus.
> When Jesus turned and saw them following, he said to
> them, "What are you looking for?" They said to him,
> "Rabbi" (which translated means Teacher), "where
> are you staying?" He said to them, "Come and see."
> They came and saw where he was staying, and they
> remained with him that day. It was about four o'clock
> in the afternoon.
>
> JOHN 1:35–39

SCRIPTURE VERSE

*"I saw the Spirit descending from heaven like a dove,
and it remained on him."* JOHN 1:32

WEEKLY PRACTICE

Consider the natural signs, symbols, and rituals of your life. Think about how they can be made even more important to enrich your life of family and friends.

Consider the Christian rituals that help you encounter God. They may include prayers, church, readings, and the use of pictures. Think about how you can make these reminders of the spiritual dimension of life more meaningful.

Born Again

> Jesus answered him, "Very truly, I tell you, no one can
> see the kingdom of God without being born from
> above." Nicodemus said to him, "How can anyone be
> born again after having grown old? Can one enter a
> second time into the mother's womb and be born?"
> Jesus answered, "Very truly, I tell you, no one can enter
> the kingdom of God without being born of water and
> Spirit. What is born of the flesh is flesh, and what is
> born of the Spirit is spirit." JOHN 3:3-8

I n the synoptic gospels (Mathew, Mark, and Luke) the
Pharisees are generally portrayed as antagonistic, challenging and looking for ways to trap Jesus, or make him appear
unfaithful to the Jewish law. Presumably they felt that if
Jesus gained too much of a following, the Pharisees themselves
might lose control over the law and its requirements. In John's
gospel, this opposition is even more pronounced so Nicodemus,
a Pharisee came to Jesus "by night," saying that no one could do
what Jesus does, "apart from the presence of God."

Jesus picks up on Nicodemus's thought, shifting from "the

presence of God" to the much more concrete "born again." Perhaps Jesus wanted to direct the conversation, taking it away from questions of the law and interpretations to more personal and spiritual dimensions.

Nicodemus, as a lawyer, takes Jesus' statement literally, responding with a grotesque image. Jesus responds with reference to water and the Spirit. We should remember that this passage is written in the time of the early church when baptism was part of the Christian culture. Just as important, for them and for us, was the theme of Spirit. In today's world, where wealth and appearance are standards by which people are judged, we have to make a daily effort to bring our minds and hearts to the realm of the Spirit.

We are more than what we eat; our lives should involve more than our work and entertainment, even more than our families and friends. We must make the effort every day to be born again: to see those around us, and the world around us with the fresh vision of a child—recently born. Children see magic everywhere; as we grow older that magic can lead to mystery, enriching our lives. Recognizing mystery does not mean turning away from the material world; rather the material world is the doorway to the mystery of God; and the Spirit opens that door.

We see rebirth around us all the time—in the growth of flowers, and fruit, and seeds that produce the next generation. We experience a mini-rebirth every day as we awaken, as the sun rises, as we take nourishment. We should not lose our appreciation for the magic of daily life; that mystery can lead us to the mysteries of the spiritual life.

In birth we were taken from a secure, peaceful, pleasant place within the womb and brought into the light and noise and demanding world in which we now live. We were, for a time, helpless. We trusted our parents and others to care for us and teach us how to care for ourselves.

Did Jesus mean to tell Nicodemus and perhaps us as well that the life of the spirit also begins with a rude awakening? Do we need to be taken, perhaps more than once in our lives, from a secure and comfortable place to a world that will demand much more of us?

The spiritual life is, however, not simply an extension of our physical lives; sometimes reversals are required. Jesus taught us that the seed must die in order for a new plant to grow. We must let die the selfish urges within us—the urges to pleasure and wealth and selfishness—if we are to be born again.

Saint Francis was caught between the demands of his father, who was a comfortable merchant wanting his son to remain secure in the family business, and the demands of the gospel. He renounced his former life completely. He left town naked, not knowing from where his clothing or his next meal would come.

In a way, Jesus was trying to be a midwife to Nicodemus, helping with his spiritual rebirth. And so we too are called upon to help nurture the Spirit in one another, so that we are reborn, not only individually but also in community.

During this week, pray that the life of the Spirit within you will take over your life more and more, so that you live this new life more deeply. Remember also your own baptism. You were born again. God's love and mercy have been given to you. The Spirit of God dwells in you and that life will not be taken away. Give thanks and smile as you think of your attachment to God. Try to help others recognize that they have been born again, that they are living in a new world, with the light and warmth of the Spirit.

MENTAL IMAGE

Nicodemus and Jesus talking at night.

SCRIPTURE READING

The reading presented above reminds us of the new life and new way of living that we lead as followers of Christ.

SCRIPTURE VERSE

Jesus answered, "Very truly, I tell you, no one can enter the kingdom of God without being born of water and Spirit."

JOHN 3:5

WEEKLY PRACTICE

Consider what it should mean to be born of the Spirit.

WEEK

10

Fully Human, Fully Divine

V ery often we don't understand the full significance of an event until it has passed. This happens with big events like weddings, recurring events like Christmas, and seemingly unimportant events— chance encounters or turning points for which the value keeps growing in our lives. Sometimes sickness or the death of a friend takes on added meaning with the passing of years.

We know of course that weddings are important, but the words and promises take root as time passes. In our family, as in many, Christmas is very big. It's not just the giving and receiving of gifts. The food and singing and stories and welcoming of friends and recollections of past Christmases—all of these things make the day and the surrounding days bigger in our memories than they might have been even at the time. And there are the chance meetings and encounters that we remember and talk about as the years pass. Our memories are like a family photo album. We look back at pictures and see new meaning.

Some of these things happened in the life of Jesus Christ.

47

People knew that he was changing their lives and their world. His teaching, his compassion, his intimate connection with God, and finally his self-offering were there for all to see. Jesus allowed those closest to him to gain a deeper insight into his work and his life. But still it took time for it all to sink in—to the lives and minds and hearts of those who wished to follow.

We know that the earliest Christians, in their prayers, called upon Jesus using the same words that they used for God; they called Jesus Lord and Savior. They also believed strongly that only God saves. So they contemplated not only the teachings and great works of Jesus but also who he was. In what way, they asked, was he connected to the God whom he called Father?

As years passed, some suggested that Jesus was the firstborn of creation—a creature but greater than all other creatures, more closely connected to God. Others said that would still make him a creature. And so in praying to and worshiping Jesus Christ, Christians proclaimed and decided that he was, in some way beyond our imaginings, with God—even before his life on earth.

This is what we believe: that God is spirit, existing beyond space and time. We are meant to share in this existence. Jesus, the Son of God, is himself part of that existence, outside of space and time.

This week pray for help that you might accept the great mystery of Jesus Christ into your life more fully, as truly divine. He is the one who can save; he can lift us beyond ourselves, beyond the world we know and outside of time—to live in the life of God.

> Let the same mind be in you that was in Christ Jesus,
> who though he was in the form of God,
>   did not regard equality with God
>   as something to be exploited,
> but emptied himself,

> taking the form of a slave,
> being born in human likeness.
> And being found in human form,
> he humbled himself
> and became obedient to the point of death—
> even death on a cross.

PHILIPPIANS 2:5–8

And so as early Christians began to accept and believe this about Jesus, some found they could not believe that he was truly human. If he was with God then he must have had knowledge of all that was to happen, of the thinking of those around him. And so he was really pretending; he was a kind of god in human clothing.

But this way of thinking was also strongly rejected. Jesus was indeed fully human. He had to think and pray for help, choose his friends and followers, and devise remarkably poetic ways to teach his message. He was like us in all ways, save sin. He was not burdened by the weight of sin. But he suffered disappointment, sorrow, pain, and death.

It is difficult to maintain the tension of Jesus as both human and divine in our minds and hearts. Each of us is more likely to think and believe in a Jesus who is more human or more divine. It is difficult to hold on to both in our lives of faith and prayer. When I was young in the Catholic Church, there was a great deal of emphasis on Jesus as divine. And so we never considered that he wrestled with decisions and plans. Things just came to him. Of course, he taught with power; he worked miracles; he even chose Judas.

But then I discovered that even conservative Christian theologians taught that Jesus as human had to work at life, just as we do. Some taught that he had to work at understanding his own mission, even his identity. In some ways, Jesus found a mystery deep within himself, just as we do. Being fully human, Jesus did not know in advance what each person around him would do; he, like us, worked with people with all of the uncertainty that life brings.

Think this week about Jesus as fully human and fully divine. He invited others to join him, building lives of complete commitment and devotion to God. It was not easy. Many would not listen; he could not heal those of his own town because of their lack of faith; Judas turned against him—for money and perhaps because he could not accept the kingdom and the kind of God that Jesus preached. But Jesus kept inviting those around him to attach themselves to him—as branches are attached to a vine.

Jesus was not what people expected of a Messiah. Jesus is still a mystery. He is God in history but in many ways not the God we would like. He is ready to save us from violence, from greed, from idle pleasure; he will save us from our own self-centeredness. But so often it is too much for us.

MENTAL IMAGE
Jesus risen, with his followers.

SCRIPTURE READING
The following verses continue the passage that we read above. With a firm conviction that Jesus was fully human, we should now consider his divinity.

> Therefore God also highly exalted him
>   and gave him the name
>   that is above every name,
> so that at the name of Jesus
>   every knee should bend,
>   in heaven and on earth and under the earth,

and every tongue should confess
    that Jesus Christ is Lord,
    to the glory of God the Father.
    PHILIPPIANS 2:9–11

SCRIPTURE VERSE

He emptied himself, taking the form of a slave,
* being born in human likeness.* PHILIPPIANS 2:7

WEEKLY PRACTICE

Contemplate this week the Jesus Christ of history; open the gospels to any page. Read just a few verses of Jesus as he teaches, heals, and calls others to himself. Pray earnestly that you will be given the grace to accept and live the life of Jesus, fully human and fully divine.

Water

T he word "water" stands for something rich in meaning as a source and sustainer of life, and it is also a word rich in spiritual meaning. The two meanings are often interconnected, so reflecting on the word can help us unite the physical and spiritual dimensions of our lives. The second verse of Genesis says that in the beginning, "the earth was a formless void and darkness covered the face of the deep, and a wind from God swept over the face of the waters." The verse gives us a wonderful, poetic expression of God immersed in the work of creation. And from the study of evolution we know that life on earth emerged from the water. This is not to say that the author of Genesis knew anything about evolution; rather it seems there is a deep-down recognition that life springs from and requires water. In the first lines of *The Canterbury Tales*, Chaucer describes how the sweet water of April enters the roots so that flowers and plants begin to grow again.

We drink water because we need it and because, when we are thirsty, a long drink of cool water is deeply satisfying. The opposite, a dryness that we feel throughout our being, may not be terribly painful at first, but it is a reminder that we need water. Similarly, our spiritual lives need nourishing—by reading Scripture, through prayer and contemplation, and by accepting wisdom from others. These are the springs of spiritual water that sustain and revive us. The spiritual thirst for this refreshment is deep down, but unlike the physical need for water, the spiritual need can be ignored; or rather we can pour something else into our souls that will not nourish and refresh us but will at least for a time let us forget about our spiritual needs. When you take a drink of cool water today, remember your spiritual needs; reflect on the refreshment you receive from reading the Scriptures and considering the workings of the Spirit within you.

Water also cleanses and refreshes the body through bathing. The Romans constructed baths everywhere they went. They loved the luxurious feeling of water over the body. In our own world, baths and bathrooms have become sumptuous. There is a spiritual counterpart to bathing. We do need to cleanse ourselves from sin and to be wary of the sources of sin—particularly money, pleasure, and power. We do need to strip down. If we get rid of our excesses with regard to clothing, ornaments, and entertainment, we will become more ready to live out our baptism, renewing our lives in Christ. And the spiritual bath is not only cleansing, but it is refreshing, as we renew our commitment to God in love.

During this week of reflecting on water, you will find many other associations of water with the Christian life. In reading Isaiah, we find the beautiful verse: "With joy you will draw water from the wells of salvation" (Isaiah 12:3). This is an image in which salvation itself comes to us in the form of clear water drawn from deep down in the earth.

I sometimes think that each of us is a well, and down deep all the wells meet, forming a great lake of pure water; and that is God—within the soul of each of us, and also uniting us. As

Meister Eckhart has said, the soul is born in God and God is born in the soul.

We have talked so far about how water can be considered as an image of the spiritual world for each of us. But water also serves a most important communal purpose. The rains pour down, nourishing crops, fruit trees, berry bushes, and giving nourishment to all living things. The psalms and poets talk about water nourishing every root—and it does. The opposite is also true; there are few things worse than a parched, water-starved land that ultimately becomes a desert. It can happen with a people—neglecting the spiritual dimensions of their lives, they lose touch with God, lose nourishment, and perhaps become disoriented and weak.

Is that happening in our modern society? It does seem that we often turn away from what we need most; that we refuse to slake the aching thirst that is within us.

MENTAL IMAGE

Jesus talking with the Samaritan woman.

SCRIPTURAL READING

It seems that everything he encountered made Jesus think about life beyond what we see and hear and touch. His spirit was always moving toward God, and he wishes the same for those around him, for us. In this week's reading about water, Jesus promises that those who receive water from him will themselves become springs of water. Our connections with Christ the Lord make it possible to bring others closer to God.

> A Samaritan woman came to draw water, and Jesus
> said to her, "Give me a drink." (His disciples had gone
> to the city to buy food.) The Samaritan woman said

to him, "How is it that you, a Jew, ask a drink of me,
a woman of Samaria?" (Jews do not share things in
common with Samaritans.) Jesus answered her, "If you
knew the gift of God, and who it is that is saying to
you, 'Give me a drink,' you would have asked him, and
he would have given you living water."

JOHN 4:7–10

SCRIPTURE VERSE

Give me a drink. JOHN 4:7

WEEKLY PRACTICE

Write in your journal all the meanings of water in your life.
Then write how water can refer symbolically to our spiritual
needs. Write a prayer or poem thanking God for the physical
and the spiritual waters that come into your life.

Love

There are different kinds of love, but they all deserve the name, and all reflect the love of God—that is, the love that God has for us and the love we have for God.

The care from our parents was for most of us our first experience of love. Babies are totally dependent. And when that dependence is answered with food and warmth, play and teaching, the baby feels good—and so does the parent. As the years pass, children become more independent; parents are needed in different ways—perhaps they shift from being total caregivers, becoming teachers, mentors, and finally friends. But love remains throughout. Of course, it sounds easy when recounted in a few sentences. We all know that growing up can be difficult and being a good parent is challenging. And so as you reflect on these roles this week, consider how with God's help you can be more generous in your love. Even if you are not a parent, you probably have many parentlike responsibilities—in teaching or guiding children, or you may spend some of your time caring for the elderly or sick. Perhaps you care in a special way for your spouse or parents. If in some ways your attitudes do not reflect a loving heart, then try to act with greater care, and your heart will follow.

And then there is the love of friendship. This is the love in which people share common interests and activities. But there is something more. Friends share a deep concern for each other's well being. Children, young adults, and in fact all of us tend to congregate with those who are like us. We want to share something deep down within us; sometimes we are not even sure what it is—new insights into life, and hopes, dreams, and sometimes heartbreak. Sharing these things is part of what it means to love.

Then there is romance—the love that is often described in novels and movies. Romance can be enchanting to the young or to those of any age who have found something that goes beyond friendship. Something within us says we want to share our lives, our dreams—we want to have a family, to build a home.

The problem is that when romance becomes a long-term, committed marriage or partnership, some things change. It's not that we love less; but we tend to discover that our partner is human. He or she is not perfect. And the real lesson in this is that I am also not perfect. Committed love can become deeper as we, the two of us, recognize that we are imperfect; we are sinners; we hurt each other. But we are together in spite of, or even because of our many weaknesses. He or she loves me with all my faults; this is remarkable. And this is when we can be Godlike. God wants us to express our love to one in whom we recognize selfishness and pride. In these recognitions, I am simply looking in a mirror. My partner and I are not perfect; but together we have found something beyond us. The love that holds us together opens a door to everlasting love. This love can also help to purify us. As we accommodate our lives to the one we love, some of the rough edges wear away and our love becomes stronger.

Love in the Christian tradition is often associated with sacrifice, even suffering and death. Jesus submitted to the Romans;

he didn't fight, or flee, or even argue. He submitted because he saw that the only way to overcome evil is to absorb the impact of the evil. And that is love. Jesus loved God; he loved those around him; and he loved people at all times and places. His love for each of us remains.

There is finally a special kind of love in God. It is love without conditions. It is offered without hope of recompense, without thinking of mutuality. It is the love that saints have offered, seeing Christ in the poorest, in those suffering from disease, in those caught in addiction. We must pray that we can receive some small share of this love. It comes from God and increases the life of the Spirit within us.

What sacrifice might love ask of you today? It may be a small inconvenience; it may be a disruption of your plans; love may mean listening; it may mean speaking; the Spirit is within, helping us to love.

You will probably see many sights and sounds this week of people seeking love, or believing they have found love. We see these images in advertisements, movies, TV, all around us. But in many cases what these people are seeking and perhaps finding is pleasure. The pleasure that comes with love is not bad; it can be good as it binds and strengthens the ties between people. But the pleasure is a helpful add-on to the deeper emotional and spiritual bond between people. A glass of wine can be delightful accompaniment to a meal. But one who drinks wine all day is not a happy person; he or she is seeking not the joys of life but to escape the difficulties of life.

The only love that is freely given, unearned, is the love that comes from God. And this is enough because all other love is built on the love that God freely gives.

MENTAL IMAGE

Those you love, and who have a call on your life.

SCRIPTURE READING

This beautiful passage from the First Letter of John describes the ideal of love—God's love for us and our response, loving God and our neighbor.

> Those who say, "I love God," and hate their brothers or sisters, are liars; for those who do not love a brother or sister whom they have seen, cannot love God whom they have not seen. The commandment we have from him is this: those who love God must love their brothers and sisters also. 1 JOHN 4:20–21

SCRIPTURE VERSE

God is love. 1 JOHN 4:8

WEEKLY PRACTICE

Consider all of those you love, and think of ways in which you can show your love more generously; think of how to share your thoughts and fears and hopes. This kind of sharing will help you grow in love—of others and of God.

Temptation: Greed

I n today's world, we hear a great deal about concern for the environment, about helping those all over the world who suffer from hunger and disease, and about social justice. But the word "temptation" has for many of us an archaic sound, medieval perhaps. It smacks of devils and sin—and these are not part of the educated person's vocabulary.

But for this week, let us think about temptation; for you and I are indeed tempted—to evil and to sin. During the course of our reflections we will return to this word, applying it to different situations. For now, let us consider in particular, the temptation to greed.

When the rich young man walked sadly away, Jesus said, "It is easier for a camel to go through the eye of a needle than for a rich man to enter the kingdom of God" (Matthew 19:24). His disciples wondered at this and Jesus said simply that with God's help all things are possible. Perhaps he meant that only God can cure our endless desire for more.

What is greed? It is a strong desire, an obsession perhaps, for possessions above all else. The thoroughly greedy person considers money most important. He or she will sacrifice almost anything for the sake of money and wealth—it is not always money we can see but simply the assurance of accumulation, of consumerism's lure, of growing investments. This state of mind is not new, but it does seem to be more pervasive than in the past and to eclipse many other goals and motives.

There was a time when the major religions condemned usury, charging money for the use of money, what we generally call interest. It did not seem right for money to make money—without any work or service or goods involved. Those days are long past; so much so that investing—money making money with no work involved—is very highly regarded. We all want to pick a stock or a fund or even a lottery ticket that will bring us lots of money. Few of us condemn this practice anymore, but it is worth noting the change in values.

A columnist recently pointed out that money seems to challenge all other values. There was a time when those engaged in professions—medicine, for example—valued their skills and the service they provided; and they felt this value independently of money. It is said that Saints Cosmas and Damien, patrons of doctors, would not accept payment for the application of their healing arts. Sojourner Truth, the great abolitionist, would not accept payment for her talks, believing it would not be right to be paid for doing God's work.

In a similar way, those in the arts took pride in their craft—whether in music, painting, or performance—placing much less value on being paid. Those engaged in building and other crafts also found satisfaction enough in doing their work well. Of course, they were pleased to earn a good living. But they would not cut corners or in any way cheapen their work for the sake of money.

It seems now, however, that money has become the measure of everything. Medical doctors expect to be very well paid; specialists higher than the general practitioners. Those at the top of any profession expect that the amount they are paid will indicate their stature: so it is in sports, entertainment, and even non-profit enterprises.

How do we avoid the infection of pervasive greed? It takes courage, prayer, meditation, and God's help to be a Christian in today's world. An important activity in combating greed is found in sharing and giving. If we think of those in need, and if we not only think but give generously, then God will open our hearts, and the temptations to greed will lessen.

Jesus often spoke in absolute terms. If you want to follow me, he said, sell what you have, give the money to the poor, and come. He did not have the time or interest in the language of lawyers or the calculations of accountants. He left that to future generations. Some have taken his maxims literally. St. Francis of Assisi gave up everything and instructed his followers to own nothing. He was radical, in the basic meaning of the word: going to the root.

The rest of us must struggle day-by-day to tame our acquisitive instincts and resist the modern currents suggesting that our worth as humans can be measured by our "net worth." Nothing could be further from the truth. When we die, those who gather to remember us will not talk about how much money we earned or left behind. They may well talk about how much we cared for those around us and how much we gave away.

MENTAL IMAGE

The early Christians bringing their money and goods to be shared with others.

SCRIPTURE READING

This reading describes an idyllic time in the very early days of Christianity when the believers shared all their goods, devoting their lives to prayer and the care of one another.

> All who believed were together and had all things
> in common; they would sell their possessions and
> goods and distribute the proceeds to all, as any had
> need. Day by day, as they spent much time together
> in the temple, they broke bread at home and ate their
> food with glad and generous hearts, praising God and
> having the goodwill of all the people. And day by day
> the Lord added to their number those who were being
> saved. ACTS 2:44-47

SCRIPTURE VERSE

They would sell their possessions and goods and distribute the proceeds to all. ACTS 2:45

WEEKLY PRACTICE

Write down three ways in which you are inclined to greed—to care too much about money and possessions; then write three things you will do to change these ways of thinking and acting.

Redemption

The word "redemption" in the Jewish-Christian tradition is a metaphor derived from buying back prisoners who had been captured, or it referred to a change in the status of slaves—who purchased their freedom either with money they had earned or through someone else's generosity.

These are metaphors, because in Scripture it is God who redeems. The psalmists and prophets often call on God to save them individually and as a people—from oppression, from enemies, and from the evils that surrounded them.

> Into your hand I commit my spirit;
>> You have redeemed me, O Lord, faithful God.
>
> PSALM 31:5

And the prophet Isaiah considers the redemption of the nation.

> Break forth together into singing,
>> you ruins of Jerusalem;
> For the Lord has comforted his people,
>> he has redeemed Jerusalem. ISAIAH 52:9

The authors of these texts felt the need to be rescued, and they experienced God's saving presence.

For us as Christians, redemption goes to the very core of our relationship to God in Christ. Jesus Christ in his life, teaching, suffering, death, and resurrection has changed everything. We are no longer simply creatures made in the image of God; we have received a new kind of life. But still we need metaphors.

Adam in his sin insulted God and closed a door. Christ as the second Adam had to pay the price of redemption. Anselm and others of the Middle Ages expanded this metaphor, discussing how it was necessary that one of equal stature with God pay the price of redemption. Much has changed in our reading of Scripture. There are very few texts or places in Scripture that call for appeasing an angry God. God does not need to be reconciled or appeased; God is like the father in the parable of the prodigal son who waited with love for his son's return. It is we, the sons and daughters, who must be reconciled. We have wandered.

Yet we can say, in metaphor and symbol, that God was touched and moved at the extraordinary faithfulness and total unselfishness of Christ the Lord. God's love in Christ and Christ's total commitment overflow throughout the world. And so all humanity, you and I, are changed, are redeemed. We can leave our sinful lives behind; we can escape the bondage of evil.

More importantly, Christ, who belongs to and is part of the eternal God, entered into creation. Through that act, all people and all of creation are brought into the family of God. Even those who have never heard of Jesus Christ belong to God in a new way. They can find God—in their families, their work, their suffering. This is not metaphor. Christ is in creation; we have a chance to bring him to others and to meet him in others each day.

What does this mean for you and for me? How do we, each day, begin anew our redeemed lives in Christ? The answer is easy and it is difficult; it is both simple and complex. What we are to do is before us.

We do not wait for redemption. We have been redeemed. And yet we continue to fall; and through our falls we come closer to understanding that God is all that matters. Life has been changed. God's love enters into our souls. All we must do is recognize and accept who we are. When we accept God's love, our actions will change. The love of God flows into us and out from us.

People of modern times have lost touch with some of the traditional images and connections with God. But redemption remains a recurring theme in literature and film. Those who have betrayed others, or themselves, often find redemption through acts of self-giving and sacrifice.

In *Les Miserables*, acts of theft are paid for with suffering far beyond what justice might require; and acts of generosity yield benefits above reasonable expectations.

In the Christian tradition there have been times when the church seemed to promote the idea that we must pay back for our sins, with repentance and acts of heroic sacrifice. While these teachings were well intentioned, it is important to remember that we do not save ourselves. Redemption comes through Christ our Lord. God accepts the great works of Jesus and, with him, God accepts us.

The message of God's saving work in Jesus has been passed down through the generations and ages. We are redeemed as individuals and also in community.

While Paul preached earnestly and forcefully, he also saw himself as connected to the tradition, then only a generation old. Christ died for our sins. More importantly, he rose from the dead. He appeared to Peter and to others. This was a real historical event, but it also takes us beyond history, into the realm of God who is both creator and redeemer.

MENTAL IMAGE

Jesus Risen, looking gently and calling to us.

SCRIPTURE READING

Paul preaches that Christ died for our sins, the apostles and others are witnesses, and we can say with Paul, "by the grace of God we are what we are."

> For I handed on to you as of first importance what I in turn had received: that Christ died for our sins in accordance with the scriptures, that he was buried, and that he was raised on the third day in accordance with the scriptures, appeared to Cephas, then to the twelve. Then he appeared to more than five hundred brothers and sisters at one time, most of whom are still alive, though some have died. Then he appeared to James, then to all the apostles. Last of all, as to one untimely born, he appeared also to me. For I am the least of the apostles, unfit to be called an apostle, because I persecuted the church of God. But by the grace of God I am what I am, and his grace toward me has not been in vain. 1 CORINTHIANS 15:3–10

SCRIPTURE VERSE

By the grace of God I am what I am, and his grace toward me has not been in vain. 1 CORINTHIANS 15:10

WEEKLY PRACTICE

Thank God for the great works of Christ and how God loves us as a mother loves her newborn, not because of anything we have done, but because we exist, and because we are one with Christ, who is risen.

Death

As I write this, the thought of death has been forced on me. Why is it that death, which is as natural as breathing, is so difficult to accept? You and I know with absolute certainty that we will die; and yet we find it most difficult to take this universal fact into our minds and hearts without trembling and saying, "yes, but not now."

Within the past few years we have lost relatives, close friends, and of course we read or hear every day about lives lost needlessly in war, through crime, and in many other ways. There was a time not long ago when death was much more present to everyone. Half of the babies born died within a few years. Sicknesses that are now treated often led to death. And people generally died at home surrounded by family. Were people in those days more able to accept death? Perhaps, but based on the literature it seems that death was always a mystery, difficult to reconcile with our deep-down desire to live. There were some who, based on their last words, seem to have been resigned. Gerard Manly Hopkins, the Jesuit priest and poet's last words were, "I'm so happy."

Jesus describes a person looking toward retirement. The man tells himself that he will put aside a great store of grain and whatever else he might need, and then enjoy a life of leisure. But

God says to the man, "This day I require your soul." So we should think about living this week and each day of it as if death awaits us. This frame of mind does not mean that we drop everything and head for church or pray all day long. It means rather that we engage ourselves in the moment, living with love and concern for others, in a way that we would be happy to call our final day.

Recently there have been references, based on a movie, to a bucket list of challenging or exciting things to do before death. But is this what life is really about? We live in a world in which excitement, novelty, and money are prized. And it is not easy to escape the climate that celebrates these things. Those with whom you talk in the course of this week and the popular media you encounter will be forcing you to ask yourself: What have I done that is special? What new places might I visit? Whom do I know who is famous? But these things are not what life is about.

What should retirement mean? How should we, retired or not, prepare for the end? Your friends and those you trust are probably not asking you about your life of prayer or the peace of soul you have achieved through meditation. But these are areas to consider as we live a life that will end. The quiet moments of reflection will make your spirit more ready for the conclusion of this journey. They are much better preparation than skydiving.

Can we ever become at peace with the thought and expectation of death? I think we can, probably not by dwelling excessively or morbidly on our own death but by looking to Christ Our Lord, remembering that he was truly human. He was a young man, gifted in understanding God's ways and the history of his people as he worked to understand his mission. He found that doing God's work in his life would require an early and violent death. The Letter to the Hebrews tells us that in his suffering, "he learned obedience" (5:8).

When transfigured before three of his disciples, Jesus glowed with the glory that God bestowed on him because of his total commitment and total engagement with God. He had recognized and realized a life beyond death. "Life beyond death" does not mean simply "life after death," or "going to heaven." It means that here and now we can live in a way that recognizes and helps others recognize that there is a spiritual and an everlasting dimension to everything we do. This is how Christ lived.

So it must be with us. If we truly believe that our life forever with God has already begun, then death is not to be feared. Life will be changed, not taken away. As Christians, we do not simply reconcile ourselves to the inevitability of death; we welcome it as the fulfillment of that total union with God for which we are created.

MENTAL IMAGE

Your own death, and the joy of union with God.

SCRIPTURE READING

In this reading, Jesus gives his listeners a short, graphic lesson about life and death.

> Then he told them a parable: "The land of a rich man produced abundantly. And he thought to himself, 'What should I do, for I have no place to store my crops?' Then he said, 'I will do this: I will pull down my barns and build larger ones, and there I will store all my grain and my goods. And I will say to my soul, Soul, you have ample goods laid up for many years, relax, eat, drink, be merry.' But God said to him, 'You fool! This very night your life is being demanded of you. And the things you have prepared, whose will they be?' So it is with those who store up treasures for themselves but are not rich toward God." LUKE 12:16–21

SCRIPTURE VERSE

And if I go and prepare a place for you, I will come again and will take you to myself, so that where I am, there you may be also.
JOHN 14:3

WEEKLY PRACTICE

Think and write in your journal what you would do differently if you knew you were to die in a year? in a week? today?

The Stranger

I n the story of the Good Samaritan, a lawyer asks Jesus what he must do to gain eternal life. Jesus tells the story of a man who is robbed, beaten, and left to die. A priest and Levite see the man and pass by. But a Samaritan, a member of a group that did not socialize with Jews, stops and ministers to the man, taking care of him, tending his wounds, and bringing him to an inn where he can rest.

The passage begins with questions. Questions play a central role in human life. They are required for survival. Questions have given rise to science, philosophy, art, and literature. We wonder what and why and how—about the world and about ourselves; and so we ask.

Karl Rahner, one of the great theologians of the last century, said that the human person is a question. He didn't mean simply that we are curious, wanting to learn. He meant that we are connected to a mystery deep within our hearts and souls. It is a mystery inviting us and connecting us to one another; a mystery that asks much and promises much. We call this mystery God. God is far beyond our comprehension. And yet we are sharing now in the life of God—as individuals and as community.

After Jesus tells the lawyer that all of the law is summed up in the directive that we love God and love our neighbor, the lawyer asks Jesus a second question, "Who is my neighbor?" and Luke the Evangelist says that he asked, "wanting to justify himself." But we, and others down through the centuries, have also asked this question.

We know that we are called upon to help, to serve, to minister. We try to do our best for those in our families, our extended families, our friends, those in our church group or community. But what are the limits? The history of peoples and religions depicts more walls to separate one group from another than bridges to connect.

In this context, the parable might have startled Jesus' listeners. It was one from the other group, the stranger who helped the one in need. We are told that Jews and Samaritans did not socialize together, were not friendly, and did not pray together. But this was the one who ministered with great care to the man who had been robbed and beaten.

And so the neighbor, in contemporary terms, turns out to be The Stranger—the one who is ethnically and religiously different.

And yet the literature and sacred writings and teachings of the different traditions tell us that ministering to the stranger is important in each of the world religions.

Hinduism teaches that all life is sacred and that all religions contain paths to God. All peoples are part of one family. Just as one individual cannot grasp the mystery of God, so neither can one culture or religion. We are, Hinduism teaches, part of one global family, and so there is no Stranger. We belong to one another. And just as members of a family should be kind and loving, so also being connected to one another should be at the foundation of all our relations, and we should renounce all forms of violence.

Buddhism goes beyond Hinduism in teaching that the distinction between groups, and even between ourselves as individuals—is an illusion. Just as the tree is nourished by the soil, sun, and rain, so we as individuals are intimately connected to our world and to one another. And the leaves, which are the children of the tree, can also be considered the parents, because through the leaves the sap, the life blood of the tree, is renewed each year. So it is with individuals and community. We are nourished by community, and we are responsible for building up community.

Judaism finds care for the stranger, the other, deeply embedded in its sacred writings and traditions. The Book of Leviticus says that "the stranger who resides with you shall be as one of your citizens, you shall love them as yourself, for you were strangers in Egypt" (19:34). Many of us remember times when we needed help in a foreign country, and it was there. Perhaps in a medical or financial emergency, or simply not knowing the way—and someone was there to help. When the Rabbi Hillel was asked to recite the entire Torah standing on one foot, he said, "What is hateful to you, do not do to others. That is the whole of the Torah, the rest is commentary."

For *Christians*, the parable of the Good Samaritan captures the full spirit of ministering to the stranger. It is echoed throughout the gospels and other writings. As God is love, so we are to love one another. In the last judgment scene of Matthew's gospel we are exhorted to care for the sick, the hungry, and all of those in need. In doing these things, we are ministering to Christ himself.

Finally, *Islam* in the Koran teaches that believers should, "serve God...and do good to...neighbors who are near, neighbors who are strangers, the companion by your side, the wayfarer that you meet." In other words, we should place no limits on our concern and ministering.

MENTAL IMAGE

Consider the man who was robbed, beaten, and left for dead.

SCRIPTURE READING

The reading tells us that we can best help one another if we purify our own thinking.

> "But a Samaritan while traveling came near him; and when he saw him, he was moved with pity. He went to him and bandaged his wounds, having poured oil and wine on them. Then he put him on his own animal, brought him to an inn, and took care of him. The next day he took out two denarii, gave them to the inn-keeper, and said, 'Take care of him; and when I come back, I will repay you whatever more you spend.'"
>
> LUKE 10:33–35

SCRIPTURE VERSE

"Which of these three do you think was a neighbor to the man who fell among robbers?" LUKE 10:36

WEEKLY PRACTICE

Consider those groups of individuals whom you tend to judge harshly. Think about your own faults. Think about the good that results from simply not judging others.

The Triune God

As Christians, we believe in the Trinity. Some say this borders on polytheism—with three persons. Others say belief in the Trinity keeps us from idolatry because we retain a sense of deep mystery in our approach to the divine. In practice, I think most of us do not often reflect on the Trinity, and we hear few sermons on this mystery. But the Trinity is part of our Christian tradition, and whether or not we reflect on it, God—one in three—is present and at work deeply within us, and also far beyond us. We should therefore strive to better understand what we believe; we should nourish this presence and our response.

For most cultures and I think most people, thoughts and feelings toward God begin with a sense of the power and beauty beyond us, and the order of the universe. We are subject to the threat of storms, disease, and wars. So it has always been; we look to God for help. We are captivated by a sunset, the vastness of the ocean, a flower, and the orderly randomness found in evolution. We trust that the sun will rise as it does each day, that the seasons will turn, and that our hearts will keep beating. And we cannot help believing there is something more, beyond what we see and feel.

All these things we read and reflect on in the psalms.

> O Lord, how manifold are your works!
>   In wisdom you have made them all:
>   The earth is full of your creatures.

PSALM 104:24

We are led, by the great figures of years past and also by our inner being, to recognize a greater truth and a greater mystery— beyond ourselves and beyond the natural world. We believe in one God. Jesus has taught us to call on this God as a Father. The God in whom we believe is the foundation, the ground—the one who holds all being together. And so we pray, not so much to ask for health and deliverance but rather that we might live in harmony, at one with God. We acknowledge that there is something more, that we are not alone, that this world and our lives have direction and purpose. We ask God for guidance.

And God our Father has already answered our prayer, sending and selecting the God-man, Jesus Christ our Lord, as our guide. And what does a guide do? The guide in an art museum points out the use of color, perspective, and connections among the figures, and perhaps he or she helps us gain a deeper appreciation of the beauty around us. Guides in historic places help us understand how we are both alike and different from those who came before us. Guides in nutrition and exercise help us develop and maintain health, strength, and physical well-being. In your spare moments today and this week, consider the different guides in your life and how much they have helped you.

Christ Our Lord is also a guide. In some ways he is similar to guides we described above and in some ways different. As we read the gospels we are often at a loss to understand how this applies to us. Jesus does not speak in half measures,

If your hand causes you to sin cut it off.
Sell all your possessions and give the money to the poor.
Take up your cross and follow me.

These and dozens of other exhortations invite us to see our lives, our world, our possessions, our work, and our friends in new ways. The words and stories of the gospel strike deeply into our hearts. This is God speaking to us. Jesus is the Word of God, spoken from all eternity, and in time speaking to our world— and now speaking to you and to me.

Jesus is our guide in words, but not only in words. He is also a guide in the example of his life. Personal relationships were important to him; he valued friends; but he was committed to something beyond this world. There are a number of gospel stories of Jesus at meals, talking about the meaning of life and how to turn ourselves toward God. He seems to have cared very little about acquiring things—or appropriating the signs of success. And yet he closely observed those around him—their work, their concerns, the good and the bad in their lives. Jesus bids us follow, even in suffering and death.

As we watch Jesus and listen to his message, where do we find the courage to really follow him?

The Word of God in Jesus speaks to us. But the words are like seeds. They require soil that is ready—a willing mind and a warm heart. This is where the Spirit of God is active. The Spirit gives light to our minds and strength to our hearts, making us ready, helping us to accept Christ into our lives and to understand what it means for us to accept and to follow. Jesus promised the Spirit, and the Spirit is with us.

Just as each breath renews, cleanses, and refreshes our blood, so also we need the Holy Spirit to be with us every moment, restoring our energy. Jesus promised to send the Spirit to remind us of all his teachings. And he has sent the Spirit—not only to the disciples gathered on that first Pentecost, but to all of us as church, and to each of us as individuals. The Spirit speaks deep within our hearts and souls. If we accept the Spirit, our lives in God will be transformed. We will live with God—in our hearts and minds, when we wake and when we fall asleep, when we talk to others, when we work, and when we are entertained. During this week, think and pray quietly that the Spirit of God will be more active in your life—bringing understanding and love to everything you do.

God is far beyond our comprehension. We experience the immense power and wisdom of the Father in all of creation. We are guided by the life, by the teaching, and by the example of the Son. We receive the light and strength to accept God in our lives through the gift of the Spirit within us.

MENTAL IMAGE

The disciples on that first Pentecost, given strength, wisdom, and love by the Spirit.

SCRIPTURE READING

In the Gospel of John, Jesus tries to explain the great mystery of the Trinity to his followers.

> "If you love me, you will keep my commandments.
> And I will ask the Father, and he will give you another
> Advocate, to be with you forever. This is the Spirit of
> truth, whom the world cannot receive, because it nei-
> ther sees him nor knows him. You know him, because
> he abides in you, and he will be in you."
>
> JOHN 14:15–17

SCRIPTURE VERSE

The grace of Our Lord Jesus Christ, the love of God, and the communion of the Holy Spirit be with all of you.

2 CORINTHIANS 13:13

WEEKLY PRACTICE

Think about how the power God has overwhelmed you and how you have sought God in times of difficulty; write about the teachings and actions of Jesus that have most affected you. Pray that the presence of the Spirit might become stronger in your life.

The Poor

Pope Francis, in *The Joy of the Gospel*, asks the question, "Why is it not news when a poor and homeless man dies, but it is news when the stock market drops two points?" It is a question worth pondering.

The question leads to broader considerations, some of which the pope also discusses. Have we as a society, perhaps as a world community, become the slaves of economic growth and even of money itself? Economic growth is indeed often talked about as an end in itself. The economic life of a nation or of the world is not a zero-sum game, we are told. Everyone's wealth can grow. Growth is good. Is it? But at what cost to other areas of life should we foster economic growth?

The reality seems to be that unlimited growth is rarely a good in itself, in any area of life; witness cancer as the extreme example: cells grow and they kill. In the Old Testament, money is not seen as an evil in itself. But judgments are made about how it was acquired and how it is used. Wealth is often created through the exploitation of the poor, or the environment, or workers, or all of these. Whether in factories, mines, farms, or retail selling, those in charge generally want to maximize profits, and this often means cutting pay, benefits, or taking shortcuts.

The rich and powerful gain at the expense of the poor and pow-
erless. Wealth seems to have become the measure of everything.
Being an artist or scientist, doctor or teacher, has value in itself.
Those who have devoted their lives in these areas are not to be
measured by the money they earn or accumulate. Their worth is
seen in their contributions they make to the lives of others. They
should be careful, as we all should, of making money and wealth
the measure of success.

How are we to think and how are we to act regarding the
poor? As Christians we want to follow the teaching and example of Christ Jesus, who repeatedly warned about the dangers of
wealth and pointed to the poor as being better off than the rich.
In his own life he seems to have cared nothing for wealth or
what wealth brings—comfort and prestige, for example. Wealth
is therefore viewed in the gospels as a hindrance. The poor are
better off because they are unencumbered.

> As he was setting out on a journey, a man ran up and
> knelt before him, and asked him, "Good Teacher, what
> must I do to inherit eternal life?" Jesus said to him,
> "Why do you call me good? No one is good but God
> alone. You know the commandments. 'You shall not
> murder; You shall not commit adultery; You shall not
> steal; You shall not bear false witness; You shall not
> defraud; Honor your father and mother.'" He said to
> him, "Teacher, I have kept all these since my youth."
> Jesus, looking at him, loved him and said, "You lack
> one thing; go, sell what you own, and give the money
> to the poor, and you will have treasure in heaven, then
> come, follow me." When he heard this, he was shocked
> and went away grieving, for he had many possessions.
>
> MARK 10:17–22

There are several ways of interpreting the story as we Christians try to work out our loyalties and reconcile our worldly interests with the gospel. One can take the story absolutely literally, like Francis of Assisi, and give up everything. He lived a life of extreme poverty—in clothing, food, and living quarters; he owned nothing and wanted his followers to do the same. It is perhaps for these reasons we consider St. Francis a most Christ-like person.

We can also consider the story as indicating levels of commitment as Christ's teaching is lived by different people and communities. The encounter of Jesus with the rich young man is a challenge for us individually and collectively. We should also note that Jesus does not say simply to walk away from your possessions or leave everything to your children or family, he says to give the money to the poor.

In the Gospel of Luke, Jesus says, "Blessed are you who are poor, for yours is the kingdom of God."

In Matthew, Jesus says, "Blessed are the poor in spirit, for theirs is the kingdom of heaven."

These verses are worth pondering for a week or more than a week. Are the poor somehow better off than the rest of us? How are they blessed? Perhaps if we consider the other extreme, of wanting to be rich—and this is a common desire in our world—we might gain additional insights. The person whose happiness depends on riches will never be happy, because he or she will never be satisfied. The wealthy generally end up measuring themselves by others who are wealthier, and there is never enough. Adequate housing, clothing, and food are not in question. It becomes important to be seen as special. One's wealth becomes the measure of one's worth, even if it is modest in comparison with others. And this is how we turn away from God and all that is good.

Another important reflection regarding poverty and the poor is "giving to the poor." In giving to the poor we should not only think of our generosity, giving of our excess, but we should give from those things we like, and the things that comfort us. If we have not worn a sweater or jacket for two years, we should probably give them away, even if we rather like them and are even attached to them. Clearly, we do not need such articles of clothing. And there are many who could use them. It is funny how we can be attached to clothes we never wear. But the opposite is also true: when we start giving things away, we find there is joy in it—in simplifying our lives and in the hope that we are helping someone else.

Becoming poor and somehow at one with the poor is for most of us a lifelong effort, but it is worth it. We will free ourselves from so much that keeps us from our engagement with God. This week take time to consider your possessions, your wealth, and what you can do for those in need.

MENTAL IMAGE

Jesus talking with the rich man.

SCRIPTURE READING

Read again the verses quoted above.

SCRIPTURE VERSE

> *"Blessed are you who are poor,*
> *for yours is the Kingdom of God."*
>
> LUKE 6:20

WEEKLY PRACTICE

Find a way to do something more for the poor, near where you live or farther away.

Do Not Worry

"Look at the birds of the air; they neither sow nor reap
nor gather into barns, and yet your heavenly Father
feeds them. Are you not of more value than they? And
can any of you by worrying add a single hour to your
span of life? And why do you worry about clothing?
Consider the lilies of the field, how they grow; they
neither toil nor spin, yet I tell you, even Solomon in all
his glory was not clothed like one of these. But if God
so clothes the grass of the field, which is alive today
and tomorrow is thrown into the oven, will he not
much more clothe you—you of little faith."

MATTHEW 6:26–30

These are among the most quoted and most beautiful words of Jesus, or of anyone. They give us much
to ponder. We might first consider what they tell us
about Jesus.

Jesus had the temperament of a poet. He saw things as they
are, and he also saw beyond them. He connected life experiences
in new ways. And he always saw connections to God. Jesus knew

what it was to work. In growing wheat, the farmer has to sow the seed, reap the harvest, and store the grain. Jesus talked about all of these things in other parables and sayings. So he was not telling his followers not to work. He marveled at the birds—their freedom, grace, and beauty. He knew that they also work for their food—searching and finding, and bringing home what is needed. But they do not worry, lose sleep, or trouble themselves wondering where their next meal will come from.

So Jesus tells his followers and us not to worry. It will do no good. Worry, tearing up our emotions with endless replaying of our finances or work problems, will not help. Like the birds, we have today to deal with and it is enough. Jesus, of course, says it with greater power—you cannot add an hour to your life by worrying.

Jesus was a psychologist. He knew that his words would not be easy to live by. So he repeats the message in different forms. Look at the lilies. Look at the flowers all around you. Jesus saw God caring for the birds. He saw the lilies coming from God. We, with our knowledge of evolution and biology and botany… we have so many explanations of nature that we easily forget about God—who is beyond and also within all of nature.

It has never been easy for people to put their lives in the hands of God. And so Jesus ends with the challenging comment, "You of little faith." He knows how difficult it is to give up worrying, to trust and to believe.

Being anxious about our finances and our investments is not only a distraction from our lives of faith and our service as Christians, it is a compromise with what Christ asks. Living with divided hearts we become like Matthew at the counting table, holding on to his money while considering Jesus' invitation to follow. Jesus is calling each of us to full, total, uncompromising commitment.

As I write this, I recall that yesterday the newspaper listed the best books of the year. One of these, a true story, was about a family, parents and two children, who were on vacation. It was the day after Christmas, the mother stepped out on the balcony. Looking at the ocean, she felt that something was strange. A few moments later the tsunami struck. The father and two children died; through some miracle, the mother lived through it. The book contains a good deal of rage. Why do such things happen? Was a loving God watching and caring? How do we reconcile our belief in a benevolent God with nature that seems so capricious and unconcerned?

Jesus was not naïve. He was not blind to the evils around him. His cousin and mentor, John the Baptist, was taken into custody and brutally murdered. The Romans had a vicious side to their occupation. They were quick to punish and even to crucify. Jesus knew this. So what did he mean telling those around him that God would feed and clothe them?

Jesus saw beyond. Looking at the birds and flowers, he saw the love and care of God. Looking at suffering and even predicting his own terrible death, he saw only his total commitment to God and to whatever might follow from that total commitment is God's work.

God is working with us; creation is unfinished. Evolution is a mighty and beautiful design. The universe has unfolded gradually, building a foundation and then adding to it, little by little.

And what about the tsunami? Death will come for each of us. The death of one close to us is always painful. The suffering and death of a child is most difficult to bear. There was, we know, a time when half of the children born died as infants. I'm sure that the losses even then were very difficult. Now we live in a different time. We expect more. We expect our children to live, to thrive.

We know that problems, pain, and difficulties are part of every life. They sometimes challenge our faith. But we have the example of Jesus, the Lord. He lived completely in God's love and yet suffered a brutal, early death. We also have the assurance that comes with community. We are not alone. We must care for one another, particularly in times of suffering and death.

MENTAL IMAGE

The birds of the air and the flowers.

SCRIPTURE READING

Read again the verses quoted above.

SCRIPTURE VERSE

Can any one of you by worrying add a single hour to your span of life? MATTHEW 6:27

WEEKLY PRACTICE

Think about your greatest worries. Consider God's loving care. Pray for the help you will need today to be more single-minded in your commitment to the gospel. This will make you less anxious about the demands of the day.

WEEK

20

Forgiveness

Jesus frequently teaches about and expresses God's forgiveness—in his interactions with people, in parables, and in brief sayings. "Neither do I condemn you. Go your way, and from now on do not sin again" (John 8:11). The lengthiest and perhaps most beautiful expression of God's compassion and forgiveness is contained in the parable of the prodigal son in Luke, chapter 15.

It is presumptuous to try to retell the stores that Jesus told. They are so perfect. But we live in a different age and perhaps a different expression can offer new insights.

> A man had two sons. The older son finished college and went to work for his father, who was a general contractor, building houses. After the younger son had graduated from high school he told his father that he wanted to go on his own and make movies, and he wanted his share of the family business and the money his father might spend on college. The next day the father gave his younger son $200,000. The younger son traveled, first to Europe, then to India, then to

South America. He had a blast. He stayed in the best hotels and ate in expensive restaurants. He went out with more girls than he could count. He gambled, and bought crazy things he didn't need. Finally, two years later, in Mexico, his money ran out. He had nothing and had to pick through garbage dumps trying to find something to eat.

Then he said to himself—am I crazy? I could at least go back and beg my father to forgive me. I did an awful thing. Maybe I could work on one of his construction crews. He is good man; he might take me back, just as a laborer; I could rent a room somewhere.

So he hitchhiked back to the States. His father heard from friends that his son was on the way and had borrowed money to take a bus for the last part of the trip. The father ran to the bus station to meet him. His son got off the bus, crying. "Father," he said, "I did an awful thing, forgive me." His father hugged him and said, "This is the happiest day of my life. I thought you might be dead. You are back. Come home! We are going to have a very big party for you."

Would you or I treat a wayward child like that, after he or she had squandered a great deal of money? Or would we put some pretty strong conditions on that child's reentry into the family? It's hard to say.

But Jesus is telling us that the love of God is so great and the compassion of God is so wonderful that if we just return, we are welcome. We are all prodigal children. We have wandered off, forgetting about God or at least not giving God the full attention that we should. God wants more from us and God waits.

But there are other sayings of Jesus in which he warns us of the importance of forgiveness. "If you are about to present your gift in the temple and remember that you have harmed a friend, leave your gift and go to make peace." This is like walking out in the middle of a church service to ask forgiveness.

And in the Lord's Prayer, Jesus tells us to pray that we will be forgiven "as we forgive others." Jesus insists that we mirror the same generous spirit that we find in the father, in the story.

There will be times during this day when you can offer forgiveness. Counselors warn us that even from a human perspective we should not let days and months or years go by, harboring grudges. It is not good for the soul. Ask God to help you forgive. You will find that great weights are lifted from your shoulders.

And if another person does harm to you or talks meanly about you? Let it go. Overcome it; don't return evil for evil. Who knows? Perhaps the simplest word can help turn a frown into a smile. Forgive. Jesus forgave even his torturers and executioners.

Peter once asked Jesus how often he should forgive—even up to seven times—thinking he was being very generous. And Jesus told him to forgive seventy times seven times. That is a lot.

MENTAL IMAGE

The younger son returning and being welcomed by his father.

SCRIPTURE READING

There is an important second meaning in the parable of the prodigal son. It is that we should not be upset or disappointed at the extraordinary goodness of God, or at things we don't fully understand.

> "Now his elder son was in the field; and when he
> came and approached the house, he heard music and
> dancing. He called one of the slaves and asked what
> was going on. He replied, 'Your brother has come, and

your father has killed the fatted calf, because he has
got him back safe and sound.' Then he became angry
and refused to go in. His father came out and began
to plead with him. But he answered his father, 'Listen!
For all these years I have been working like a slave for
you, and I have never disobeyed your command; yet
you have never given me even a young goat so that I
might celebrate with my friends. But when this son
of yours came back, who has devoured your property
with prostitutes, you killed the fatted calf for him!'
Then the father said to him, 'Son, you are always with
me, and all that is mine is yours. But we had to celebrate and rejoice, because this brother of yours was
dead, and has come to life; he was lost and has been
found.'" LUKE 15:25–32

SCRIPTURE VERSE

"Forgive us our sins as we forgive those who sin against us."
MATTHEW 6:12

WEEKLY PRACTICE

Think quietly about those you should forgive. Perhaps someone
has failed to repay money borrowed. Perhaps someone has done
a mean thing to one of your children or a close friend. These
things are very hard to forgive. We should also remember that
after Jesus forgave, he said, "Go and sin no more."

If you feel so moved, write to someone this week. Let them
know that you care about them; thank them for what they have
done in your life.

Sharing Meals

B ody and spirit are intimately intertwined in each of us. Special occasions are celebrated with meals—a wedding, birthday, Christmas, anniversaries. When I was growing up, our family ate dinner together every night at six o'clock. Generally, we had meat, potatoes, and a vegetable, and fish on Fridays. We talked about our friends, school—mostly the little things in our lives. In that way, we knew each other. In the family of which I am father we also ate together every night—our two girls, close in age, shared stories about friends, activities, and teachers. We talked about events, the world, places we had visited, our plans for the future. We strengthened the bonds by caring about and for one another.

Unfortunately, many families no longer share regular meals. Time, work, activities, TV, and other distractions have conspired to prevent family meals. People eat at different times or while watching television or on the run. There is no need to assign blame, but something is lost.

During this week, I am trying to pay closer attention to meals. I suggest that you do the same. Food selection and preparation are important. Paying attention to the quality of what we eat is a way of paying attention to the quality of our lives. If you do very little in meal preparation, you might be more attentive to the eating itself. Try to better engage in the taste and texture, the color and aroma of each food. Enjoy how the flavors blend. If you do some part of the preparation for some of the meals, the opportunities are endless.

Meals can be an important aid to our growth as Christians; they were significant in Jesus' life. The first of his miracles, as described in John's gospel, was to turn water into wine—to save embarrassment to his host and, perhaps, his mother who had invited Jesus and his friends, and they may have helped create the shortage.

After Matthew's call to follow Jesus we are told that he held a dinner party for his friends and for Jesus and his followers. At another dinner party, Jesus berated his host for not showing him the common courtesies expected when entering a home. At the same meal, Jesus allowed a repentant woman to wash his feet with her tears. He seems to have been a regular guest at the house of his friends Mary, Martha, and their brother, Lazarus. And there were many other meals for Jesus and his followers. We can only wish they had written more about the food and conversations they shared.

A recurring theme in Jesus' teachings is reciprocity. As we forgive others or show mercy to others, so God will forgive and show mercy to us. And yet, paradoxically, Jesus also teaches that we should not do good to others in order to be recognized or receive some kindness in return.

> He said also to the one who had invited him, "When you give a luncheon or a dinner, do not invite your friends or your brothers or your relatives or rich neighbors, in case they may invite you in return, and you would be repaid. But when you give a banquet, invite the poor, the crippled, the lame, and the blind. And

you will be blessed, because they cannot repay you, for
you will be repaid at the resurrection of the righteous."
LUKE 14:12–14

Not many of us will take this teaching literally. Dorothy Day and
others who have opened places for the hungry and poor to eat
have done important work, feeding those in need. It is for each
of us to decide how we can share meals with those who do not
have enough.

There are many dimensions to meals. Sometimes we dine
alone; perhaps, if you live alone or because of family circumstances, you often dine alone. In fact, it is helpful for all of us on
occasion to eat alone without the television or radio. Taste the
food; consider the many people who have made this meal possible. They include farmers, perhaps migrant workers who picked
and collected fruit and vegetables. Bakers and others prepared
the bread and packaged it. Trains and trucks brought the food
to the stores where you purchased it. Consider the wonderful
way in which spices and cooking enhance the flavor and nutrition of food. If you look online for a simple recipe, you will find
dozens of interesting ways to prepare a dish. We should try to
consider ourselves as part of a connected world—in eating, and
in hunger.

In Matthew's gospel we read that the crowds followed and
listened to Jesus for three days. And his teaching so captivated
them that they forgot even to eat. But Jesus did not forget, and
in his compassion he made it so that seven loaves and a few fish
fed the crowd of four thousand.

Paying closer attention to the food we eat makes us more
aware of who we are; our lives become more complete. Fast food
not only inhibits digestion; it also puts our lives into a pace that
is not mentally or spiritually helpful.

This week pay closer attention to meals.

MENTAL IMAGE

Jesus sharing a meal with his friends.

SCRIPTURE READING

Consider this reading from the Gospel of Matthew and how you can help those who do not have enough to eat.

> Then Jesus called his disciples to him and said, "I have compassion for the crowd, because they have been with me now for three days and have nothing to eat; and I do not want to send them away hungry, for they might faint on the way." The disciples said to him, "Where are we to get enough bread in the desert to feed so great a crowd?" Jesus asked them, "How many loaves have you?" They said, "Seven, and a few small fish." MATTHEW 15:32–34

SCRIPTURE VERSE

"I have compassion for the crowd, because they have been with me now for three days and have nothing to eat; and I do not want to send them away hungry, for they might faint on the way."
MATTHEW 15:32

WEEKLY PRACTICE

During the first part of the week: Pay special attention to what you eat and how you eat. Take your time.

During the second half of the week: Pay attention to your conversation at meals, trying to help those around you experience the goodness of God in their lives.

The Eucharist and Community

I t is unfortunate that the Bread of Life, given for us, has become a sign and source of separateness rather than of community and union. This separation is made explicit in church documents.

> Because Catholics believe that the celebration of the Eucharist is a sign of the reality of the oneness of faith, life, and worship, members of those churches with whom we are not yet fully united are ordinarily not admitted to Holy Communion.
>
> **UNITED STATES CONFERENCE OF CATHOLIC BISHOPS, 1996**

Going back to the beginning, we find that unity and community were viewed as integral to the Eucharist. Jesus in his Last Supper discourse in John's gospel speaks of the vine and the branches. We who believe, who partake of the bread, are all attached to him. We need Jesus and we belong to one another. The Didache, perhaps the earliest catechism, written at about the same time as John's gospel, speaks beautifully of the individual grains becoming one bread, as a symbol of the church.

> As this broken bread was once scattered on the mountains, and after it had been brought together became one, so may thy Church be gathered together from the ends of the earth....

Saint Augustine reflects on the mystery of Christ's presence in the Eucharist, comparing it to his presence in us, the body of Christ, as described by Paul.

> So now, if you want to understand the body of Christ, listen to the Apostle Paul speaking to the faithful: "You are the body of Christ, member for member" (1 Corinthians 12:27). If you, therefore, are Christ's body and members, it is your own mystery that is placed on the Lord's table! It is your own mystery that you are receiving!...Be a member of Christ's body, then, so that your "Amen" may ring true! But what role does the bread play? We have no theory of our own to propose here; listen, instead, to what Paul says about this sacrament: "The bread is one, and we, though many, are one body" (1 Corinthians 10:17).
> AUGUSTINE, SERMON 272

Fast forwarding to our day, we find that we are heirs of the Reformation, with varied teachings about the Eucharist—real presence, transubstantiation, symbol, sign, remembrance. In addition, we live in a secular age in which traditional structures are fragmented. Attending Mass and receiving Communion do not mean what they once did. What can be done to regain a sense of community and purpose, and somehow connect these to the Eucharist?

First, more than ever, we need prayer and meditation. As Catholics we have come to appreciate the central role of sacred Scripture in faith and the use of our own language in worship. In this, we have accepted several important Protestant contributions. As we meditate on verses and situations in Scripture, we should be grateful for the work of scholars and of all denominations who, working together, have increased our understanding and insight into the Christian message.

We might also seek out interfaith activities. For more than ten years I have participated in Bible discussions with a group from Catholic and Protestant traditions. When we disagree about the meaning or relevance of a text it is rarely because of our different traditions. We agree on the essentials. We nurture one another's faith. But we are still separated by that one core essential that is the subject of this week's reflections—reception of the Eucharist.

The area of service is also important and perhaps instructive. For more than a year, members of our parish, working with others in the community, have sponsored an immigrant Syrian family, helping them settle into the community, get started in school, go through the various medical and green card requirements, and in general take their first steps in a new life. In this case we all work together without much thought or comment about our religious beliefs and how they flow into our actions. But they are there.

What can be done about the Eucharist? It seems an intractable problem; and yet, I don't think it should be.

We might reflect on several suggestions of Catholic theologians. Monika Hellwig said in reference to the Eucharist, "What happens to us is more important than what happens to the bread." This gives us pause. It is almost shocking. I think many of us, growing up as Catholics, really did think that the "miracle" of what happens to the bread was more important than receiving Communion. The bread becomes something divine, the God-man among us. This belief is an important part of our tradition and can bring us closer to God. But anything to do with the Eucharist should also bring us closer to one another in community, partaking of the one bread. Jesus said, "Take and eat."

We might also consider the words of Karl Rahner, who said that we of the Christian traditions should declare unity and then work on the details. So simple and yet daring! Might we not consider starting with the great sign of unity? Might something happen, something good, if we were to act as if we were one? Perhaps we could at least attend one another's church services from time to time, while discussing what to do about communion.

Finally, I am completing this reflection on the feast of the Epiphany, remembering and celebrating Jesus' availability to those beyond the nation of Israel. Jesus did not and does not turn people away. Like the Magi we should continue to search for the Lord. We are likely to find him in unexpected places.

MENTAL IMAGE

Jesus at the Last Supper, sharing his life with those around him.

SCRIPTURE READING

Paul's description of the Eucharist is very simple, very similar to what we read in the gospels.

> For I received from the Lord what I also handed on
> to you, that the Lord Jesus on the night when he was
> betrayed took a loaf of bread, and when he had given
> thanks, he broke it and said, "This is my body that is

for you. Do this in remembrance of me." In the same
way he took the cup also, after supper, saying, "This
cup is the new covenant in my blood. Do this, as often
as you drink it, in remembrance of me." For as often as
you eat this bread and drink the cup, you proclaim the
Lord's death until he comes.

I CORINTHIANS 11:23–26

Reflect this week on how you can reawaken the life of Christ within you and help make that life more real in the Christian communities to which you belong.

SCRIPTURE VERSE
Take and eat. This is my body.

WEEKLY PRACTICE
Look for ways during the week to better appreciate the history and religious practice of Christian traditions different from your own, or even those with different perspectives within your own tradition. Consider also what happens to you when you receive the Eucharist.

Dimensions of the Church

S ome years ago, Fr. Avery Dulles, theologian and later cardinal, wrote simply and insightfully about the dimensions of the church, using the metaphor of length and breadth and height and depth. This week we hope to gain a greater appreciation of the community of believers that is the church.

By *length*, we mean that the church has a history in time, from today going back to the earliest disciples and to Jesus himself. We could trace the lives and example of some of the saints and exemplary Christians. But instead, think about those who helped shape your own Christian life.

Think for a few minutes about your life as a child and growing up. You had teachers who were also examples of Christian living. They taught you your prayers, read and explained Bible stories, and helped you understand the words of Jesus. These people also had teachers, going back another generation, who taught and explained the gospels and Christian living as it was understood in their time. And so there is an unbroken chain, going back through the generations to the beginning, trying to grasp the surprising message that God is with us—in the person of Jesus and within our hearts and minds as the Spirit. This historical chain is different for each of us—passing through many countries, languages, and customs. Our God is a God of history, entering into the lives of those who have come before and finally entering into your life and mine. God wished to be understood in our world and in our lives even if it often means being misunderstood, as Jesus was indeed misunderstood. God wants us to live the message, not simply learn it. Catechisms are not bad. But learning from a catechism and then reading the gospels is like going from the indoors out into the sunshine. Inside, things are generally tidy and predictable; outside, a world of beauty, excitement, and the unknown awaits us.

The *breadth* of the church refers to the numbers of people who today bear the name Christian, or who are living as Christians—perhaps even without naming Christ as their model. Not very long ago, Christians of different traditions were bitterly opposed to one another—Catholic and Protestant, and even within the different sects there were major controversies. In some parts of the world there were armed conflicts between Christians.

But in recent years there has been greater harmony, respect, discussion, and prayer among Christians of different traditions. We might say it is about time—dialogue and ecumenical spirit are important. We live in a world in which many people feel they can get along fine without God; others believe that religions have caused more harm than good; and others feel that Christianity as promoted by the churches interferes with a more personal spirituality. In the face of these issues, it is important that we as Christians support one another. We have much to share. The church does indeed possess a wondrous breadth—imbedded in peoples and cultures.

The *height* of the church refers to the divine origin and that the Spirit of God remains with us, as the church. The Spirit of God gathers us together and we each have our special gifts from the Spirit.

> Now there are varieties of gifts, but the same Spirit;
> and there are varieties of services, but the same Lord;
> and there are varieties of activities, but it is the same
> God who activates all of them in everyone. To each is
> given the manifestation of the Spirit for the common
> good. 1 CORINTHIANS 12:4–7

Reading these words, you probably ask yourself about your gifts. What is the special work or activity that the Spirit has given you? Don't spend a lot of time worrying about the answer to this question. Give your life to Christ and without knowing it you will bring the Spirit to others every day.

The *depth* of the church refers to our humanity and even sinfulness. We have all done things for which we are deeply ashamed. We are selfish, vain, unkind, greedy, proud, and on and on. These faults and sins are part of our lives. Ask God to help you overcome these things, but also accept yourself, as God does.

And we must acknowledge that the church itself has shown itself to be sinful. In pride, in seeking riches, in taking advantage of the weak, in exercising power, prelates and leaders have disgraced themselves and the church. How are we to be members of such an organization? But condemning the whole church or walking away from the teachings of Christ and the support of good people in the church will not solve the problem. We are the church—now and throughout history. The church, like Jesus Christ the founder, is human and divine. Think and pray this week about all the people who have helped and continue to help you be a Christian, be a faithful member of the church.

MENTAL IMAGE

Picture all of those who have helped you become a better Christian; in your imagination surround yourself with these people, past and present, living and dead.

SCRIPTURE READING

Reread the passage above and consider how the church benefits in all its dimensions through the gifts of the Spirit.

SCRIPTURE VERSE

I pray that you may have the power to comprehend, with all the saints, what is the breadth and length, and height and depth, and to know the love of Christ that surpasses knowledge, so that you may be filled with all the fullness of God. EPHESIANS 3:18–19

WEEKLY PRACTICE

Select one of the four dimensions of the church and write about how it has been important in your life. Write a prayer thanking God for the church, with all its faults.

Original Sin

After their disobedience, Adam and Eve are put out of the garden, and God tells them that as a result of their sin they will have to work hard for their food, and that there will be pain in childbirth.

For centuries the story was taken literally and a great deal was made out of life before and after the fall, with the sense that humankind and each one of us has been damaged by that primal disobedience. Recent theologians, while discounting the Adam and Eve story as history have helped to deepen our understanding of original sin.

We are indeed born into a pervasive situation in which we are affected by evil. This is original sin. It is not something that happened long ago. It is a present condition, our condition. There are many examples of how it is impossible to escape the reaches of sin—not sins that we ourselves have committed, but nevertheless sins that reach us with their aftershocks; and they implicate us.

Suppose you purchase a computer. And suppose the workers who manufactured the computer were so exploited in a distant country that they would rather have died than continue. In fact, at some computer factories, workers have killed themselves to avoid the misery of their lives. The injustices of the process reach us. Indirectly, we support the structures that created and continue the exploitation.

As you use the computer, your browser may provide access to materials that celebrate violence and sexual exploitation. Even though you do not engage in these things, your participation in the browser helps support them.

After a few years, you buy a new computer and get rid of the old one. The old one might then make its way to a remote part of the world where it is taken apart so that the metals and electrical parts can be extracted and sold. But there is poison in those parts, and people are harmed, perhaps seriously. Again we are enmeshed in evil.

Or consider the taxes you pay. Some of the money goes for important government services—payment of retirement benefits, education, roads, and bridges. But some may go for wars you believe are unjust, or for the collection of information from citizens in ways that are contrary to our own laws. You are again caught up in a condition that is at least in part unjust. And there is little you can do about it.

Or imagine that you are hired by a big company to do satisfying work for which you are qualified. But that same company engages in some unjust practices—perhaps in manufacturing things that are known to be harmful, or in deceptive marketing practices.

You can easily think of situations in your own life that bring some remnants of sin, evil, and guilt. You might say that this is the human condition. That is the point. If you and I lived in the English colonies three hundred years ago we would be implicated in slavery. Even if we didn't own slaves it is likely we would have benefited in some way from their work.

Novels, short stories, and movies often deal with the themes of original sin and redemption, although they may not be identified as such. Consider any of the novels of Charles Dickens. There are people who are good and those who are bad; there is conflict; there is resolution. But very often there is also a web of social conditions, and that web is infected at its core by injustice, greed, and selfishness. It is the same in Shakespeare's tragedies. The love that Romeo and Juliet feel for each other is the source of their doom, because their families have been antagonistic for longer than anyone can remember. There is indeed an inherited guilt, and that guilt seems to force evil on those in its path.

But again, we wonder how God is involved in all this. We believe, based on Scripture and the constant teaching of Christian tradition, that God is good and holy and loving, and that in creating us as spiritual beings God wishes to communicate the God-life to us. But in original sin, the human race says no to this offer.

The offer, however, remains. God will not turn away. We are enmeshed in sin and complicit in a sinful world, but God, in Christ, offers redemption and new life. We have at the roots of our being the ability to say yes to God. Throughout the New Testament, Jesus and after him Paul and others talk of rebirth. We must be born again in the spirit. This does not mean we save ourselves. It means that the grace of God, working deeply within, helps us to answer and respond.

Reflect this week on the sin that surrounds us—in the world and throughout history. But reflect in confidence and love, because God's love and grace given through Christ overcome original sin.

MENTAL IMAGE

The man and the woman leaving the garden in sadness.

SCRIPTURE READING

We read over and over in Scripture that Christ has conquered sin. But still we are also told that we must strive to live as Christ wishes.

> As God's chosen ones, holy and beloved, clothe your-
> selves with compassion, kindness, humility, meekness,
> and patience. Bear with one another and, if anyone has
> a complaint against another, forgive each other, just
> as the Lord has forgiven you, so you also must forgive.
> Above all, clothe yourselves with love, which binds
> everything together in perfect harmony.
>
> COLOSSIANS 3:12–14

SCRIPTURE VERSE

And let the peace of Christ rule in your hearts.   COLOSSIANS 3:15

WEEKLY PRACTICE

Consider the ways in which you are affected by, and even complicit in, sinful situations; and how you can lead a more Christ-centered life.

Work

Throughout history, work has been an essential part of life. In the second creation story of Genesis we read that even before the fall, "The Lord God took the man and put him in the Garden of Eden to till it and keep it." And until a few hundred years ago work was largely physical—farming, building, making tools, caring for the children, cooking, and making clothes. These things are what the large majority of people spent most of their time doing.

St. Benedict, the founder of western monasticism, offered the motto "to pray and to work" to his monks. It was the focus of their lives. In those centuries, the importance of work was more apparent than it is to us. But work is still relevant, even indispensable. We work in order to earn money; and that money pays for a place to live, for our food, for our many needs and wants. But we also feel that work should be satisfying and enriching—to ourselves and to others. Young people spend time searching and preparing for the right career.

Even now as you read this, you probably find your mind slipping to the work you have to do. You may feel you are well paid or not well paid; or perhaps you are not paid at all. But the work is there. It is an important part of life. For this week,

I suggest a few things to consider about your work and how you approach it.

First if your work is worth doing, it is worth doing well, conscientiously, and carefully. Some years ago I visited Japan and found something very noticeable about the Japanese approach to work. I spoke with someone who had spent time in Japan, and he had the very same impression. It is this: the Japanese do their work with total commitment. Taxi drivers, servers in restaurants, office workers, and others do their work as if their lives depend on it. They attend to every detail of the job—with care. I guess it is something in their culture and training. This is how they do things. (Of course cultures change, and the Japanese may not be as conscientious as they once were.)

As honest people and as Christians, we should try to be conscientious in our work. There are standards of excellence in every job and profession. Whether you are caring for children, preparing a marketing plan, selling merchandise, or teaching, there are ways to do your job with attention and care. We all hope and trust that those who worked to make our clothes, our homes, our computer programs did these things well and that the products reflect a commitment to excellence. We hope that our children's teachers are fully committed to their work. Think this week about your own work and whether you are giving it full attention and care.

The second area I would suggest regarding work is that we take care about honesty. We live in a culture that expects and often condones cutting corners. Whistle-blowers exist because it so often happens—in manufacturing, in advertising, in government work, even in teaching and learning—that dishonesty enters into the project as a way of increasing profits, or pretending something is more than it is, or even in wanting to pass a test. Consider this week whether you are honest in your work, or whether you are participating in things that are unjust or unfair.

What can you do about it?

A third area to consider regarding work is how we talk with and about our coworkers. There are many opportunities to help, perhaps to mentor or to assist those with whom we work. There are also many occasions in which we might diminish those around us or gossip about other people. We have to examine our consciences about these things. There are so many opportunities to do good, we should not let them pass.

In much of work there is drudgery, and sometimes what seems worse than drudgery. We have to follow orders and do things according to the boss's way, when we may have a much better idea. What is to be done? Accept the Spirit of God into your life, into your work. God's Spirit will give you strength, and with that strength you will be able to imitate Christ Our Lord in your work and in dealing with those around you.

Paul the apostle after his conversion spent his time tirelessly preaching the gospel of Christ, and yet he mentions his work—he was a tentmaker—and that he continued to work hard "so as not to be a burden to anyone." He worked and he encouraged others to do the same.

So it is with us. Work gives us a sense of satisfaction and independence. Work is an important source of confidence and self-esteem. The money should not be the main thing. We should take pride in the skill and care that go into our work; where possible, we should be enterprising and creative in our work.

This week consider all the different dimensions of your work and how your work can increase your union with God.

MENTAL IMAGE

Paul the apostle making a tent.

SCRIPTURE READING

> For you yourselves know how you ought to imitate us;
> we were not idle when we were with you, and we did
> not eat anyone's bread without paying for it; but with
> toil and labor we worked night and day, so that we
> might not burden any of you.
>
> 2 THESSALONIANS 3:7–8

SCRIPTURE VERSE

*The Lord God took the man and put him in the garden of Eden to
till it and keep it.* GENESIS 2:15

WEEKLY PRACTICE

Think about your work. Consider how you can do your work
with greater care and even love.

WEEK

26

The Holy Spirit

The Holy Spirit is the energy of God within us—as individuals and as community. The first disciples, after living close to Christ, listening to his teachings, and wanting to follow him, were nevertheless lost and frightened after his death. Even after his resurrection and the assurances he gave that their work was just beginning, they huddled together—uncertain.

The Holy Spirit came. And they were changed—individually and in community. They saw the world in a new way. Everything remained—family life, work, leisure, and all their inclinations for good and ill—and yet everything was changed. It was now God's world in which they lived. It was a world redeemed and renewed and looking forward to the completion of the kingdom. And so the church took shape. Unfortunately, there have been many relapses along the way. Some say Christianity has failed; others that it has not really been tried. We who believe are trying to make room for the Holy Spirit—in our lives and in our world.

The Acts of the Apostles repeatedly describes the work of the Holy Spirit in those wonderful early days of the church. The Spirit came first through Jesus, then through Peter's preaching,

115

and then seems to be poured out, sometimes independently of the Apostles. On one occasion Peter is surprised that the Spirit is a step ahead of him.

> Then Peter began to speak to them, "I truly under-
> stand that God shows no partiality, but in every nation
> anyone who fears him and does what is right is accept-
> able to him. You know the message he sent to the
> people of Israel preaching peace by Jesus Christ—he
> is Lord of all. That message spread throughout Judea,
> beginning in Galilee after the baptism that John
> announced: how God anointed Jesus of Nazareth with
> the Holy Spirit and with power; how he went about
> doing good and healing all who were oppressed by the
> devil, for God was with him." ACTS 10:34-38

Peter goes on to say that the waters of baptism cannot be with-held from those who have received the gift of the Holy Spirit.

We need to enkindle this sense of surprise in our own lives of faith. We do not control God or the gift of the Spirit. God through the workings of the Spirit is among us. We need to open our minds and hearts, to be surprised—by the workings of the Spirit within us and by the presence of the Spirit in others.

The gifts of the Spirit can be seen in the goodness and gener-osity of those who give selflessly, whether in the name of Christ or not. Christian charities do outstanding work for those in need—refugees and those stricken by war and famine. But so do secular agencies, working to help the same people. We do not control the Spirit of God. Christians who are scientists collabo-rate with others to better understand environmental problems and issues of health and disease, and to seek possible solutions. Christians pray together with those of other religions in the firm belief that the one Spirit is with all of us.

Sometimes the Spirit takes us out of our comfort zone, to use a contemporary expression. Consider Peter, who had a dream or vision in which he was told to eat all kinds of animals that were considered unclean and forbidden by Jewish law. He said that he could not do it. Three times the voice tells him that he should eat "What God has made clean" (Acts 10:15). Peter was profoundly changed and understood that the Gentiles did not have to become Jews to follow Christ. We take this for granted. But what are the challenges in our day? In what new ways is God asking you and me to look at the things of this world? What people or ways of life have we been slow to accept? The Spirit of God is present in people and cultures and events beyond our power to understand.

But there is evil in the world. There is indeed, and we must ask God to send his Spirit to help us discern, to help us be more generous in every way. Greed, envy, laziness, pride, and all the vices surround us; these evils are even within us. But the grace of God is far stronger than these enemies of God.

In these weekly reflections, we are trying to let the Holy Spirit come more fully into our hearts and minds and souls. Like Peter we can be instruments of God's love. The Spirit of God wants to work through you. In conversation, in your work, in your encounters with friends, you will bring God's love and hope to others.

MENTAL IMAGE

Peter preaching with the energy of the Spirit.

SCRIPTURE READING

> While Peter was still speaking, the Holy Spirit fell
> upon all who heard the word. The circumcised believ-
> ers who had come with Peter were astounded that the
> gift of the Holy Spirit had been poured out even on
> the Gentiles, for they heard them speaking in tongues
> and extolling God. Then Peter said, "Can anyone with-
> hold the water for baptizing these people who have
> received the Holy Spirit just as we have?"
>
> ACTS 10:44–47

SCRIPTURE VERSE

*While Peter was speaking the Holy Spirit fell upon all who heard
the word.* ACTS 10:44

WEEKLY PRACTICE

Several times each day, as time permits, sit quietly, and for
three to five minutes pay attention just to your breathing. As
you breathe in, think of the Holy Spirit coming deep into your
being; as you breathe out think of worldly cares leaving you.